£5-99

To a

Gurdjieff in Action

Gurdjieff in Action

J. H. REYNER

London
GEORGE ALLEN & UNWIN
Boston   Sydney

First published in 1980

GEORGE ALLEN & UNWIN LTD
40 Museum Street, London WC1A 1LU

© J. H. Reyner, 1980

British Library Cataloguing in Publication Data

Reyner, John Hereward
    Gurdjieff in action.
    1. Gurdjieff, George
    I. Title
    197'.2   B4249.G84   80-40886

    ISBN 0-04-294117-2

Set in 11 on 13 point Baskerville by Grove Graphics
and printed in Great Britain
by Biddles Ltd, Guildford, Surrey

Contents

Illustrations

Extract from the Liber Mutus
of 1718 depicting Angels
attempting to awaken
sleeping humanity

Foreword

The now familiar ideas of the Russian mystic George Ivanovitch Gurdjieff have particular significance today, for there can be no doubt that the world has entered the age of barbarism foretold in legend; and conventional remedies are clearly inadequate. It was, in fact, a deep mistrust of orthodox doctrines which prompted the youthful Gurdjieff to forsake his home at the age of fifteen and embark on a long and arduous quest for sources of ancient wisdom which could reveal the real purpose of life on earth.

The journey was to last for twenty years until he finally found what he sought in a Sufi monastery in the Hindu Kush. He realised that the evils of the present age arise from the fact that humanity is spiritually asleep – an idea expressed by Christ nearly two thousand years ago, but hardly ever understood – and he devoted the rest of his life to the attempt to arouse a proper awareness of man's place and purpose.

His teaching was no new religion promising some future and automatic salvation. On the contrary, it requires a sustained individual effort to become more conscious of one's behaviour in the midst of the daily activities of the present life; so that it is sometimes called the Fourth Way, as distinct from the ways of fakir, monk or yogi which require a withdrawal from the world.

Originally the ideas were communicated personally and secretly, but after Gurdjieff's death in 1949 a number of books began to appear, notably P. D. Ouspensky's *In Search of the Miraculous* which is recognised as the definitive exposition of the teaching, and an extensive series of *Psychological Commentaries* by Maurice Nicoll (under whom I studied for fifteen years). In addition there was released an allegorical tale of man's situation entitled *All and Everything* which had been written by Gurdjieff himself as a cosmological background to the ideas.

The real value of the teaching, however, lies in its application, by which one can learn how to make conscious use of the experiences of life. If this can be achieved it begins to inspire one's whole existence with a kind of impersonal delight; but even more significantly it contributes to the pool of cosmic consciousness and thereby helps to offset the forces of evil which are evoked by the greed and selfishness of sleeping humanity.

This is an unfamiliar idea but one finds many references to the positive and apparently disproportionate influence of individual awakening. In particular, there is a legend attributed to Gautama Buddha concerning a Bodhisattva (enlightened being) called 'The Regarder of the Cries of the World'. Suppose, says the legend, thousands of people, going about their normal occupations, are suddenly assailed by storms and malevolent demons, if just one of them remembers the name of this Bodhisattva, then all the people will be delivered from peril.

There is an urgent need at the present time to remember one's real purpose. Influences from more conscious levels of the Universe are continually playing upon the earth but we are too concerned with our personal desires to hear them. The inspiration of Gurdjieff's teaching lies not in its detailed formulations but in its power to stimulate the development of individual consciousness. This is the theme of the present book which is based on a series of talks given to a group at Berkhamsted.

I

The Mystery of Life

We live in what the eminent astronomer Sir James Jeans called 'a mysterious Universe'. To the scientist it does indeed appear so, because the more one discovers of its intricacies the more elegant are the designs which are revealed. To the ordinary man or woman, however, involved in the plot and counterplot of the day's events there seems to be neither time nor inclination to give undue thought to the workings of what appears to be a relentless and demanding existence.

Yet Albert Einstein, surely no idle dreamer, was very aware of the need for wonder. In his book *The World as I see It** he says, 'The fairest thing we can experience is the sense of the mysterious. It is the fundamental emotion which stands at the cradle of true art and true science. He who knows it not, who can no longer wonder, no longer feel amazement, is as good as dead, a snuffed out candle'.

The sense of wonder, in fact, has for many of us been lost. We had it as children, when we understood much more than we do now, before we were hypnotised by the false gods of material progress. To some extent this is necessary in a civilised society and some people regard it as the only practical pursuit. There are many, however, who accept the challenges of life as a necessary and even stimulating activity without believing that

* Citadel Press, Secaucus, N.J.

this is the whole purpose of existence; in which case the many mysteries become a source of inspiration.

A mystery is customarily defined as something hidden or inexplicable, but the word has a deeper and unsuspected significance because it is derived from a Greek root meaning to close the eyes. Hence there is the striking implication that the truth is hidden *only because we will not look for it.* We go through life with our minds firmly closed against anything which we do not immediately understand.

Yet in our secret heart we know that there are intelligences in the Universe incomparably superior to the limited intellect of everyday life. It is to these that we must look for the keys to the mysteries. It is said, indeed, that we have a right to demand them. But we have to learn how to make the demand; and it starts with the re-awakening of the sense of wonder.

Nature itself is a great mystery, of which we are sometimes faintly aware. There is today such a wealth of information in popular literature and TV programmes that one can hardly fail to be intrigued by the infinite variety and beauty of the various forms of life. If it occurs to us to wonder how it all came about we are told that all these forms evolved from simple prototypes through a succession of entirely accidental mutations. Those which provided some advantage survived, resulting in the development over millions of years of the vast elaboration of life today.

Our interest is aroused by the ingenuity of these developments; but it is a superficial interest. Do we really believe that it all happened by accident? Is there not behind this bewildering variety a mind and a purpose? There is, indeed, evidence of the existence of directing intelligences which control the behaviour of particular species, which psychologists call 'group minds'. To take a small example, how does a new-born spider know how to spin a web, without instruction from parents it has never seen? You may say that the appropriate programme has been laid down in its genes, but this is merely an explanation of the mechanism involved. Who laid down the programme, not just for spiders but for the whole structure of organic life; and for what reason?

What, in fact, is the purpose of this complex film of living matter that covers the surface of the earth? One can accept it as simply part of the natural environment; but since we are ourselves involved in it we should find it more meaningful if we could discern its real function. To do this, however, we must look beyond the evidence of the senses. Our knowledge of the world is primarily derived from the five physical senses. We learn by experience to interpret the information which they supply by building up patterns of associations which determine our reactions, and our behaviour in general.

Yet science tells us that these senses are curiously limited in perception. There are many sounds which our ears do not detect, while our eyes respond to less than one trillionth of the vast spectrum of electromagnetic waves known to science; and there are other influences not perceived by the ordinary senses. Hence it is clear that the world we know is merely a tiny fraction of a vastly greater *unmanifest* world.

This idea of an unmanifest world is of enormous importance. It is, in fact, the essential key to the mystery of the Universe. But this invisible background is not just an extension of the physical world. It is a realm containing vibrations and energies of an entirely different order from those perceived by the senses. In religious parlance it is called Heaven; but it should not be thought of as an isolated and remote state. Esoteric legend tells us that the Universe comprises a hierarchy of world-orders created by a Supreme or Absolute Intelligence as a living and evolving structure.

These world-orders are not physical though some of their activities create the appearances of the material world. They should be envisaged as patterns of possibilities which are brought into being by the intelligence appropriate to the particular level. The affairs of our planet are administered by a very lowly world-order, nearly the lowest in the structure. It is, nevertheless, a highly intelligent creation of which the physical attributes perceived by the senses are a mere shadow. It is a structure which is required, in its own vast period of time, to grow in stature so that its energy may be returned to the Source.

For this to happen, however, it must be able to receive influences from higher levels, for which purpose there has to be a suitable medium through which these influences can be transmitted. This is the function of the strange phenomenon of organic life. We can understand this to a small degree in physical terms. In the absence of vegetation the energy from the sun on which the earth depends would be reflected uselessly (as it is from the moon). The film of organic life entraps the energy and passes it into the earth.

The unmanifest earth is subject to far more subtle influences which are received by the psychological aspects of organic life, including man who has a particularly important role to play in the scheme. These influences are of a quite different quality from those which direct the physical behaviour of the world, and it is with these conscious influences that esoteric teaching is concerned.

It is clear, therefore, that organic life is not just an accident as the scientists seem to think. It has been created for a specific purpose which we shall try to understand, and is directed by an intelligence of a high order. It is characterised by ceaseless activity for which again there is a significant reason. Any natural system tends to degenerate into a condition of quiescence in which there is no energy available for useful work – a condition known as maximum entropy. Nature therefore arranges that all living creatures are obliged to make constant effort for survival and the energy so expended maintains organic life as a whole in a suitably active condition for the exercise of its required functions. Effort, indeed, is a fundamental requirement in the Universe, and it is a sombre thought that the misplaced

4

idealism of today which attempts to make life uniformly easy is reducing humanity to a state of spiritual impotence.

Now while these ideas may be interesting they appear to have a somewhat remote and academic quality. Do the widely varied and often beautiful manifestations of life on earth exist solely for the benefit of a vast and impersonal Universe which has been slowly evolving over millions of years, and will presumably continue on its relentless course for countless more aeons? If so, what is the situation of man who lives in and is part of this structure? Is he, as some people believe, no more than a highly-sophisticated animal who has developed unusual faculties and powers but is individually of negligible importance?

This is not an acceptable idea because we have an innate conviction of a significant individual destiny, which is reinforced by the fact that man is clearly equipped with superior faculties – in particular, the ability to think and reason and to experience emotions as distinct from sensations. Animals, and even plants, have feelings and in some cases a limited power of reasoning, but these are instinctive reactions resulting from conditioned responses to external stimulus. Man is distinguished by the possession of an individual mind which enables him to interpret his experiences more consciously.

As a result he has been able to establish over the ages a considerable degree of communication with his fellow beings. He has observed and recorded the behaviour of his environment in detail and has built up a prodigious library of knowledge. His emotional perceptions respond to the more elusive values of truth and beauty which have inspired the great works of art and music, of poetry and literature, of discovery and adventure, which have provided us with such an invaluable heritage.

All this is surely something extra. Despite his arrogance man is physically a very small part of the whole structure of organic life which would appear to fulfil the requirements of cosmic evolution quite adequately. Why then is there any need for the creation of man, with his superior powers – which indeed he often appears to use in a very irresponsible manner?

Here, for us, is the great mystery which we must try to elucidate if we are to make proper use of the life we have been given. For a while we are allowed to take things as they come, but having established ourselves in life we have to begin to ask questions, and seek understanding. Now, we have seen that life in general acts as a medium for the transmission of extra-terrestrial influences. Esoteric legend says that man is a special creation provided with a range of extra potentialities, not merely in respect of his intellect. It says further that these faculties, if properly exercised, can extract from the kaleidoscopic situations of life a certain refined form of energy which is as nectar for the gods. In these terms man is by no means of negligible significance. This is indeed the sole reason for his creation; but there is no occasion for conceit because most of us not only fail to make use of these extra faculties but are not even aware that they exist.

2

What is Man?

Of all the remarkable phenomena in the world around us the one we take most for granted is man himself. This is probably because we are completely engrossed in meeting the inexorable demands of life. As such we do no more than contribute our quota to the ceaseless activity which organic life requires to sustain its operations.

Yet man is a superior species endowed with more than the mere ability to conduct himself in life. He is distinguished from the animals by possessing an individual mind – an intelligence in the unmanifest world which directs the behaviour of the body. This means that, contrary to his customary belief, man is not only his body which is no more than a very clever mechanism for carrying out the directions of something of a higher order.

Maurice Nicoll used to say that this was the first great mystery about man, namely that he is in two parts, spiritual and temporal. The temporal part is his physical body which is a vehicle in which he can travel through the phenomenal world. It is provided with a range of senses which receive impressions from the environment, and it includes a remarkable computer called the brain which analyses and interprets the information in accordance with patterns of associations established by instinct and experience.

The aggregate of this vast array of associations and attitudes

7

constitutes what we call our Personality and this determines our behaviour in the constantly changing situations of life. But although we speak of *our* Personality it is not really our own. It is an acquired pattern which has been established in us by other people, by parents and teachers, or from books and illustrations, or by imitation, augmented by the developing experience of life. Most of it, in fact, has been derived from external sources and so is not really our own, though there are certain inherent tendencies which do belong to us.

What then, if anything, is real? It is the spiritual part of a man which exists in the unmanifest world, and as such is subject to quite different influences and laws. In particular, it is not under the laws of passing time but is, for us, eternal. Hence it must be regarded as something which is inhabiting the body for a brief spell. It is said to come down from a very high place in the Universe – a level which for us is Divine – in the course of which it becomes clothed in successively coarse materials until it finally reaches the level of earth and is housed in a physical body.

Evidently it is a many-splendoured thing having several levels of existence, which can only be dimly apprehended in their entirety. We can, however, acknowledge the presence within the body of a real, but unmanifest, spirit. Gurdjieff called it Essence, which has the meaning of the intrinsic nature of anything. Essence, he said, is what is our own, as distinct from Personality which is acquired and does not belong to us.

The idea of a spirit within the body is familiar enough, but it is usually merely an abstract concept. Can we actually feel the presence of this spiritual element as a living part of our being? It is clearly unmanifest, that is to say not evident to the physical senses, but even this we interpret inadequately. We know that the senses are extremely limited in their perception so that we can understand intellectually that there is a part of the body – and perhaps quite a large part – which is invisible.

But this is *not* Essence. We tend to think of Essence as in some way an attachment to the body whereas it is actually an entity of an entirely different nature, composed of material of a higher order in the Universe, material of incomparably finer quality than the body which it inhabits. For this very reason the sense-based mind has difficulty in understanding what it is like. As the deeper, more intuitive levels of the mind develop we begin to see something of its real nature but in the meantime we can appreciate that, because it is real, it must be simple in character, uncluttered by the complex associations of the Personality.

Ouspensky records an experiment which Gurdjieff conducted in his group on one occasion. There was a man who had a very active Personality; who had strong opinions about everything, and was always ready to talk about them. Gurdjieff, with his superior mind, was able to render this Personality temporarily quiescent, leaving only Essence; and the man changed completely. He was no longer anxious to talk about anything. He did not want to give any opinion, but just wanted to be himself. He was pressed to say what he would like and after a little time he said, 'I would like some raspberry jam'.

This sounds ludicrous, but actually it was a memory of a pleasant taste; and taste is an instinctive sensation as also are scents and textures. They are real and connect directly with Essence, uncontaminated by judgments and attitudes, and we have all experienced occasions when some random taste or scent will awaken long-forgotten memories. Essence, in fact, has the simplicity of a young child, responding to influences of truth and beauty, and particularly of harmony because it understands relationships in the unmanifest world to which it belongs. But like a child it has to grow up and is often lazy.

This idea is a surprise to conventional thinking which assumes vaguely that the spirit, whatever it is, must already be fully developed. But if so, why is it necessary that it should enter a physical body? Here lies the mystery. Physical man strutting so blithely on the earth is little different from the animals which he treats with such condescension. Both live by associations, some instinctive, some acquired. In man these are more highly developed owing to his ability to reason, but each serves organic life in its appropriate sphere.

However, we are told that man is a special creation designed to serve as an intermediary between the physical and spiritual levels in the Universe. But for this purpose to be fulfilled a certain kind of effort is necessary. So Essence is deliberately created *incomplete* – a self-developing organism capable of growing in stature provided that it can receive suitable nourishment; and in so doing it generates a refined quality of energy which is of special value to the higher levels.

This is why man is provided with a spirit. He is often likened to a seed which is required to burgeon and bear fruit. The whole object of the sojourn on earth, in fact, is to promote growth of Essence; and it should be noted that in so doing a man serves something higher than himself.

How does Essence obtain the nourishment it requires? It has come down to the level of earth where it is provided with a physical body. This is a truly remarkable mechanism brought into being and sustained by a part of the impersonal intelligence of organic life as a whole. This provides the programmes of response to stimulus to which the body reacts automatically. But the presence of Essence within the body permits a more significant programming by the creation of an individual mind. Its first task is to adapt itself more meaningfully to the environment, for which purpose the brain begins to form associations and assemble them in such a way as to contend successfully with the situations of life. This is the formation of Personality, which is meant to be a preliminary operation consciously directed by the mind.

But Essence goes to sleep. The behaviour of the body appears quite satisfactory and becomes automatic, requiring no conscious attention; in the absence of which the undirected brain begins to form a whole range of spurious associations – associations built on self-love, greed, desire, self-esteem, pride, vanity and similar criteria, and the behaviour quickly becomes entirely dominated by this False Personality. But Essence is real. How can it derive any nourishment from the activities of False Personality? They are so unreal, so invented, that they are utterly useless as food; and so Essence starves.

Fortunately it is not abandoned by Heaven, which is well aware of the difficulties. Hence it provides powerful influences to remind Essence of its purpose. You will recall the illustration in the *Liber Mutus* which depicts a man asleep on the ground with angels blowing trumpets to pierce his slumber. If Essence hears these calls it begins to arouse the deeper levels of the mind which can provide altogether more significant interpretations of events.

Every event involves the expenditure of energy which is used mechanically by life; but if the activity can be undertaken *consciously* the quality of the energy is changed and it becomes acceptable food for Essence. For a long time we do not understand what is meant by conscious participation in events because we believe that we are already fully conscious. Actually we have very little control over the events of the day which dissipate our energy for cosmic requirements. If we could see events as part of a pattern in which we are participating we would begin to use this energy for our own needs. This is called 'going to the day', and the energy saved not only nourishes Essence but invigorates the deeper levels of the mind which can create even greater awareness; so that the effect is cumulative.

We begin to create new associations which have superior possibilities. They permit us to make use of the wonderful machine with which we have been supplied instead of allowing it to run riot without attention. Personality can then be used as it was intended to be. For example, the activities of a true craftsman are food for Essence because they are real. The simple delight in doing something well involves no self-merit, no expectation of reward. We quickly contaminate it with the taint of self-satisfaction and vanity, but the initial delight is a positive emotion and is quite real.

So this is the task. We have to substitute understanding for mere knowledge. The idea that man is a self-developing organism can be a purely intellectual concept which the conventional mind may regard as a mere theory, possibly of doubtful validity. The intuitive levels of the mind know that it is true, and are able to understand the dual nature of man which we have been talking about. If I can begin to experience the sense of awe and wonder at the existence of this mystery in myself I may begin to feel the presence of Essence as a God-given and very precious gift which I want to nourish more than anything in life.

3

The Universe of Order

What do we really know of the Universe in which we spend our days? The astronomers tell us that we inhabit a somewhat insignificant planet, one of a family of nine orbiting round the sun, which is itself one of some 100,000 million stars existing at relatively enormous distances from ourselves and each other in a kind of vast disc in the limitless bounds of space. Our situation in this galaxy is near the outer rim so that we can perceive it edge-on in the night sky as a faintly luminous streak which the ancients called the Milky Way.

Nor is this the whole, for we are told that the Milky Way is only one of a further 1,000 million galaxies in the depths of space which signal their existence to us in various strange ways, not least of which is the recently discovered evidence of stars which, having come to the end of their appointed use, disappear out of our space altogether in a cataclysmic collapse called a black hole.

For most of us these vast concepts are of little significance. We are concerned with more practical issues, the inexorable succession of days and years, of the changing seasons; and though we may accept that these effects are caused by the rotation of the earth on its axis in its orbit round the sun, this is only of academic interest. We expect the sun to rise each day and arrange our affairs accordingly.

13

Yet there are legends of occasions when it did not. Do we ever feel any sense of gratitude to a Universe which provides such an ordered existence? I once read a story in which the earth passed through a supposititious region which failed to conduct any of the customary vibrations, causing a complete disruption of communication. Such was the confusion that when conditions became normal again an edict was issued requiring all newspapers and letter-headings for ever after to carry the slogan 'Thank God for light'.

Admittedly a flight of imagination, but in our preoccupation with our problems do we ever give thanks for the existence of order, or appreciate the natural rhythms which we take so much for granted? Yet life is fundamentally a rhythmic process involving expenditure of energy followed by periods of recuperation. The alternation of day and night provides the opportunity for this necessary replenishment as also, in a longer time scale, does the quiescence of winter after the activity of summer.

The behaviour of the natural world conforms to well-established laws, of which Science has discovered a great deal. Yet the very elegance of some of these laws is a clear indication of the existence of some directing intelligence; and this must of necessity be of a higher order than that of the world which it directs. We have seen that the causes of the events of life lie in the vastly greater unmanifest world beyond the interpretations of the senses; but to understand this it is evident that a different kind of knowledge will be required, derived from the much finer perceptions of the spiritual realms.

This is secret knowledge, not accessible to the ordinary intellect. Yet it is available to the intuitive mind which can respond to influences of a higher quality than the logic of life. These are called esoteric influences, meaning 'from within', and originate from beings who inhabit higher regions of the Universe. Gurdjieff called this the Conscious Circle of Humanity, which is concerned to convey the truths and relationships of the real world in language which can be understood by the mortal mind.

This is the inspiration of poets and mystics through the ages, sometimes through actual messengers who inhabit the earth for a time.

According to this real knowledge, the Universe is not an accidental structure merging into an infinite vastness. This is only the outward appearance of a living intelligence emanating from a Supreme or Absolute Being in a succession of stages of increasing complexity, each having its own intelligence and consciousness.

The various legends of the creation all interpret the Universe as having been assembled out of the void by the will of this Supreme Being. Plato, in the Timaeus Myth, postulates that by drawing apart adjacent parts of the pervading emptiness there was created a tension which could then be manifest on an increasingly coarse scale through the process of time.

A created Universe, however, must necessarily conform to specific rules. Ouspensky relates the amusing tale of a theological student who was asked if he could conceive of anything that God could not do. 'Easily', he replied. 'He could not take my ace of trumps with a two.' Every activity in the Universe is subject to appropriate laws.

These laws, of course, will be many and varied but it is said that they all develop from two fundamental principles, known as the Law of Three and the Law of Seven, which operate in an increasingly detailed manner in the successive levels. The Law of Three requires that for any effective manifestation three forces have to combine in an appropriate relationship. There is first an active force, a force of intention. This automatically brings into play an opposing or passive force, as is expressed in the well-known dictum – to every action there is an equal and opposite reaction. But this is a condition of stalemate. Only the introduction of a third, or reconciling force of some kind can resolve the impasse so that a useful action may result.

We find expression of this law in various religions, notably the Trinity of the Christian ethic or the triple deity of Hinduism – Brahma the creator, Shiva the destroyer and Vishnu the preserver. Gurdjieff illustrated its practical application in the formulation called the Ray of Creation which shows how the Universe is brought into being by the establishment of a sequence of world-orders. These should not be interpreted as material in form but rather as levels of intelligence concerned with the administration of the successive manifestations, as in Fig. 1.

The first world-order is brought into being by the combination of the three primal forces in their simplest form, and is therefore called World 3. It is the highest, most comprehensive level of created intelligence, subject only to the will of the (uncreate) Absolute. It is responsible for the direction and maintenance of all the 1,000 million galaxies in the physical Universe, but this is only a fraction of its activities, most of which are beyond our comprehension.

This responsibility is then delegated to a number of subordinate intelligences which, in physical terms, are responsible for individual galaxies. These will be brought into being by a further, more detailed application of the Law of Three, but will still be subject to the laws of the parent world-order. Hence this second order of creation is known as World 6, under six orders

World Order	Representation
1	Absolute
3	All Worlds
6	Our Galaxy
12	Our Sun
24	Planets (Astral world)
48	Earth (Phenomenal world)
96	Moon

Figure 1

of laws, three from World 3 plus three of its own.

The third world-order is concerned with still smaller units, in physical terms the individual suns in the galaxies. This will be subservient to the laws of World 3 *and* World 6, so that with the three laws of its own creation it will be under $3 + 6 + 3 = 12$ orders of laws and hence is designated World 12. We are principally interested in those aspects of the successive world-orders which relate to our particular situation. In these terms World 12 directs the behaviour of our solar system and so is often called the Sun intelligence; but this is only a small part of its functions. It is, for example, the level from which esoteric influences are promulgated.

This then creates a subordinate intelligence, which again is under twice as many orders of laws, i.e. all those of its predecessors plus three of its own, $3 + 6 + 12 + 3 = 24$, so that it is called World 24. This is for us a very important intelligence. It is concerned with the planetary system which orbits around, and is subservient to the Sun, but it has far more comprehensive duties. It contains the unmanifest patterns which are the causes of the events of the phenomenal world, and is the realm in which Essence resides, so that it is often called the Astral world.

There then follows a fifth world-order of more limited scale which by the same rules will be under twice as many laws as the Astral world and hence is called World 48. It is the intelligence concerned with the administration of the phenomenal world in both its physical and psychological aspects. This is the world which we inhabit in our daily lives and is thus of particular significance for us. It is characterised by multiplicity and impermanence. This may sound strange, but actually because it is subject to the merciless law of passing time nothing in it endures. The conditions change from moment to moment. It is a world of continual expectation, continual change of state. The physical body and the Personality are subject to the same laws, but the spirit is not.

The series concludes with a sixth world-order called World

96 which is the lowest order of intelligence still in contact with the Absolute. It is represented physically by the moon but its real significance is psychological. It feeds on the waste products of the higher levels and is sometimes called the growing tip of the Ray.

The Ray of Creation is not a static pattern, but is a representation of a living and evolving structure in which each level uses the material at its disposal to raise its stature to that of the level above. It has been likened to a yoyo flung out by the hand of the Absolute, to which it will return in its appointed time.

This concept of a hierarchy of world-orders is of the greatest importance if it can be properly understood. The development of the series by successive application of the Law of Three is an intellectual formulation which the logical mind can accept as a reasonable hypothesis. But if the idea is to have significant meaning we have to feel the reality of these world-orders as living and intelligent beings, having an actual existence, and possessing a certain materiality, though evidently of a quite different quality from that of the familiar world.

In point of fact the materiality of the physical environment is an illusion of the senses. Science tells us that all matter is composed of invisible atoms which are not only incredibly small but are separated by relatively enormous distances. They are assembled in regular patterns which interfere with the equally invisible light waves and so create the appearances of solidity and colour. Yet even these atoms are not solid particles but merely temporary distortions of the intangible fabric of the void, so that supposedly solid matter is really mostly empty space.

Evidently this basic and all-pervading fabric can be utilised in many more ways than we know of, creating other kinds of space and time. Hence the higher world-orders must be envisaged as realms having their own materiality and possessing their own intelligence and consciousness. They can be, and are, inhabited by beings of a higher order, as said earlier; but the implication of practical importance is that the spiritual part of a man can also inhabit these higher regions and it is the development of this possibility which is his principal task.

It was said earlier that influences from higher levels were transmitted to the earth through the medium of organic life. This is an additional structure which occupies a position between World 24 and World 48 in order to fulfil certain requirements of the second fundamental law – the Law of Seven, which will be discussed later (Chapter 10).

Man is part of organic life and therefore serves the level of World 48. However, this only applies to his body which we have seen is merely a vehicle. His spirit is not so confined and can serve, and inhabit, higher levels; but to do this he has to learn how to make conscious use of the experiences of life.

4

Positive Thinking

Everyone asks at some time or another why we are here on earth. Life itself does not provide any satisfactory explanation. Yet we have an innate belief that there is some purpose beyond the mere struggle for survival and comfort, and this is reinforced by esoteric legend which gives clear and unequivocal answers. It says that man is created to serve the higher levels of the Universe by conscious participation in the experiences of life. Unfortunately this does not happen because the hypnotism of events persuades people that they are already fully conscious, so that there is no need to make any special effort beyond that of going about the daily affairs of life. So influences are provided by more conscious levels of the Universe to help man to awaken. The operative word is 'help'. These influences do not in themselves produce any awakening. They can only indicate the way in which man can himself awaken, because this is part of the plan, this is the only way in which he can fulfil his purpose.

The first step is to try to see for ourselves that we are not conscious. We have to verify by self-observation that our behaviour is that of a machine which responds to the information received by the senses, which we call impressions. There is nothing wrong with this. It is not only necessary but very cleverly organised .What is wrong is that there is no conscious control of the machine. We find from experience that there is no single person or director in charge of the operations. Our behaviour is determined primarily by associations which have been acquired over the years, partly by education, partly by experience. Out of the vast library of associations the brain selects small groups which are relevant to each particular type of event, and these will fall into widely different categories. For example, the associations involved in going upstairs to bed are obviously quite different from those concerned in playing a guitar.

Now, each of these groups of associations constitutes what we might call a 'behaviour unit'. They will operate individually and automatically every time a particular type of impression is received. But we are quite unaware of this and think that it is we who have initiated the particular behaviour. So that we say 'I' to each and every one of these little automata, even though they may be quite contradictory. A small change of circumstances can produce a quite different reaction.

We are told to try to observe these many I's in our Personality and to separate from them. It is not easy because they are really little persons able to think, feel and act, using established associations in all these categories; but we have to begin to see that they are not ourselves but are only a part of the necessary mechanism of the body. However, the observation is rarely objective. We judge what we observe, we judge the behaviour of the machine; and by what standards will we judge it? If we are honest we find that we are judging the behaviour by reference to a wholly imaginary 'real' self situated somewhere behind the scenes, which knows exactly what should be done but is prevented from doing so by the failings of the flesh.

For a long time, certainly in my own experience, one has the feeling of something in the background which is really in charge but is constantly being impeded by all sorts of random events and happenings, so that we make excuses, we justify our actions; and because of this judgment we never accept what we observe. We devote our energies to trying to alter the behaviour, to change the way in which we react to the changing situations. In life this is permissible; in some respects it is even necessary. One can change one's behaviour in certain situations because it is expedient to do so. But if we do this we are only substituting one set of mechanical associations for another. The behaviour of the machine is still the result of an automatic response to established programmes, established associations, and there is no change in the level of being.

What do we mean by 'being'? Conventionally it is defined as the essential nature of anything but a more significant interpretation is to say that the being of anything is determined by its use in the Universe. In these terms it is clear that there are many levels of being. A stone has a being as part of the structure of the earth; but if it is hewn and dressed its usefulness is increased so that its level of being is raised; and still more if it is sculptured by an artist into a form which will convey impressions of beauty to the beholder. Yet none of this is comparable with the being of, say, a cow which can convert grass into food for man.

Man has a still higher quality of being, which again can be of different levels. As long as he continues to react unconsciously and mechanically to all his experiences, his usefulness is limited to the fulfilment of the requirements of life; but if his interpretations of events are related to the idea of the existence of superior levels of intelligence and consciousness the quality of his being is raised and may be of use to a higher level of the Universe – a level of intelligence greater than that of the phenomenal world in which we operate so complacently, but to which we do not belong and are only visiting.

However, there is an unsuspected trap here. Full of idealism we begin to make a variety of new aims, small and large, only to find that we are constantly failing to keep them. We are, in fact, continually missing the mark – which incidentally is the real meaning of the word sin in the Gospels – and this causes dismay and discomfort. We are told, for example, that there is an urgency in the need to awaken and that time is counted, and this makes us even more disturbed and even terrified. So we begin to develop an attitude of guilt and try to achieve our aims from this terrible driving force of sin.

Now this is negative thinking and is not only useless but dangerous. So much religious doctrine is based on this attitude of fear, which is the deepest sin. It is quite right that there should be a feeling of discomfort. We are told specifically that we have to work against mechanicalness. We have to work against the complacent state of sleep. But the change which is necessary is not a change of the mechanism, not a change of the machine. It is a change of the mind which directs the behaviour. This is what esotericism is about. It is about what Christ called *metanoia* which is change of mind. As we have already seen, all our behaviour is the result of the interpretation of the impressions received by the senses in accordance with programmes already established by the mind, and these can only be changed by a more conscious direction.

Let us see what this means. There *is* a real self in each of us but this is a spiritual entity. It is something which originates at the level of the starry galaxy, a level which for us is divine, and it comes down through the intervening levels of the Universe, being closest to us in what we call Essence. This is real, but it is required to inhabit a physical body in order to exist on this earth and it is this physical body which collects information through the senses and which translates it into action.

Can you see there are two quite clear forms of translation? All the incoming information can be interpreted purely in terms of what good it does for me. This makes a perfunctory use of the programmes which Essence laid down at our birth and leads to the development of the Personality. With this we remain content in the state of (psychological) sleep. But it is possible by the use of the deeper levels of the mind to develop programmes by which the same information can be interpreted with reference to the real purpose of existence, namely that we are here to serve the higher levels of the Universe – which as we

23

said at the outset is done by conscious participation in events. So you can see that only this spiritual part of a man can provide conscious interpretations.

Now we take this for granted, without thinking what it involves. It is something that we ought surely to ponder for ourselves because it is evident that these superior interpretations cannot possibly be provided by the Personality. This is like trying to pull oneself up by one's shoelaces or trying to lift the plank on which one is standing. It is necessary to make contact with intelligences of a superior quality from those which serve the everyday purposes of life.

This is the intelligence of Essence which, although undeveloped, is still our only contact with Heaven; and it is an intelligence of a different order. It operates in the Astral realm, beyond the limitations of passing time and so whatever programmes it provides are not concerned with progress in time, but with progress in understanding. Now this is a positive idea, an idea we must begin to put our weight into. In the ordinary way so much of our effort is concerned with result. It is concerned with making progress and this is wrong effort. Again, one must not be dismayed by this, because this is the way it has to be. We have to go down the wrong road before we can discover that it is leading nowhere.

So we have to make mistakes – but not be content to go on making them. Let us try to listen occasionally to conscious influences which have a different outlook. Emanating from above, they are looking from a different point of view, and although we may not fully understand them we can recognise their truth with the emotional mind – can feel that there are interpretations of events which are not concerned with progress in time; so that when we experience what we call difficult circumstances we see that these are to be made use of now, and no longer put all our feeling into waiting for the clouds to roll by.

This is positive thinking which can change one's outlook completely. One begins to feel part of a living and purposeful

24

Universe, which cannot be served by the exercise of Personality because this is necessarily concerned solely with the affairs of life. We can fulfil our true purpose only by submission to a higher authority, the spiritual authority of which we have been speaking; and this is something *internal,* in each one of us. Esoteric and religious teaching is designed to enable us to listen to this inner authority. But it cannot do the job for us. We have to make our own effort.

How then can we develop this ability to listen? One of the most powerful ways is the practice of what is called 'inner stop'. One can understand the idea of an external stop – remaining completely motionless, as in stalking game. Correspondingly, there is 'inner stop' which would involve a similar cessation of movement internally. It is not stopping thoughts – which in any case is impossible. If you have ever tried to do it you will have found it can't be done. But thoughts are provided by I's which are brought on the stage by the constantly changing impressions of life. We are surrounded by I's at every moment, which want to attract our attention. They want us to believe that we are them. They want to use our name and drain our force. But if we could become motionless in the mind these little I's could never find us. They would rush round seeking this self to which they want to attach themselves and would not be able to find it. This is not fanciful. You know how a bird or animal will 'freeze' in the presence of danger, not to feign death as is sometimes thought but because whilst it is motionless it cannot be detected. You can observe this with your own vision. The eyes will detect movement immediately, long before they are aware of colour or shape. Anything which is quite motionless is invisible.

Can we make ourselves invisible to the crowd of I's in our Personality which are always clamouring for attention? Yes, it is possible briefly to exercise this inner stop and for a moment one is free. We can never dispense with I's because once created they continue to exist and will always come on stage on cue. But we can stand still in ourselves so that they can't find us;

until suddenly somebody comes, or we remember we didn't call the doctor, or something like that, and immediately all these I's come in and say, 'Ah, we've got him'.

It is worth a great deal of thought to see how one could encompass this. We can start with certain I's or groups of I's which we have begun to observe as being troublesome and can just try to stand still – motionless – under the onslaught of these I's. We find that they actually lose their way, cannot find us. We are no longer in a turmoil because we have managed to remain still. We can for a moment put on our invisible hat. If we could manage to do this consistently it would be possible to become invisible at will; which would be a form of self-remembering.

This is expressed very simply in the forty-sixth Psalm in the words 'Be still and know that I am God'. One is for a moment aware of being part of the living Universe, and of one's purpose therein. There is a most inspiring passage in one of the Sutras of the Indian mystic Patanjali, reputed to be the originator of Yoga, which seems very relevant.

He says, 'We have thought of ourselves, perhaps, as creatures moving upon this earth, rather helpless, at the mercy of storm and hunger and our enemies. We are to think of ourselves as immortals, dwelling in the Light, encompassed and sustained by spiritual powers. The steady effort to hold this thought will awaken dormant and unrealised powers, which will unveil to us the nearness of the Eternal'.*

* *The Yoga Sutras of Patanjali* by Charles Johnson (Watkins).

5

The Concept of Centres

Why do we behave as we do? You may perhaps say that this
depends on one's type, but this is a very cursory answer. Most
people, in fact, are content to regard their behaviour as controlled by a vaguely-defined self which has acquired through
experience a comprehensive pattern of memory called the
mind.

This is a comfortable but erroneous belief, based on a series of
half-truths. Certainly we possess an elaborate memory-pattern
which has been built up by experience from our earliest youth.
It constitutes a vast library of associations to which the brain
refers in deciding how to react to the changing situations of life.
However, this is not the mind, which is an intelligence of a
different order, but to understand this we must look a little
deeper.

We assume vaguely that the brain receives information from
the senses, which it then uses to determine the necessary action;
but how does it do this? Quite simply, it is a highly-sophisticated
computer – i.e. a mechanism which can analyse and act upon
information supplied to it. But to do this it must have been told
how to deal with the information. To take a simple example,
suppose a computer is fed with two numbers in succession – say
3 and 5. It can add them to make 8, it can multiply them to
make 15, or it can take the first figure as a tens digit so that the

two make 35. It can do many other things, but only if it has been told what is required by an appropriate 'programme'.

This is a trivial example. The programmes required by the human brain are obviously much more elaborate, which makes it all the more pertinent to ask where they come from. You may say that they develop by experience, but this again is a half-truth, because a machine cannot programme itself. The brain has a very considerable mechanical intelligence – as indeed has the whole physical body. It can store information in a prodigious memory and it can be instructed as to how to make use of this accumulation of data, which it does with remarkable efficiency; and as part of its instructions it can be told how to amend or adapt its reactions to changing conditions so that it may appear to be entirely self-governing. In fact, all its behaviour is determined by an automatic response to established programmes, which in the first place must have been laid down by an intelligence of a superior order.

What do we mean by intelligence? Literally, the word means 'reading between', i.e. awareness of relationships; but this can operate at different levels. We have seen that behind the physical appearances of the senses there are worlds of higher dimensions which contain the real patterns of existence. An intelligence of a higher order can lay down programmes for the brain to enable it to contend with the conditions of life. Indeed this control by a superior intelligence is clearly evident in the very behaviour of the physical body which performs all its natural functions in obedience to programmes laid down at our birth by an unmanifest intelligence which we call instinct.

This is a much more inspiring interpretation of the concept of the mind. In the ordinary way the word is used very loosely and is often confused with intellect. But thought and reasoning are mechanical processes performed by the brain. The mind is a directing intelligence *in the unmanifest world,* and by that very fact can operate at many levels of increasing potentiality. Nor is it confined to human beings. The whole of the phenomenal world is directed by appropriate minds, as also are the higher world-orders in the hierarchy of creation at their level, all subject to the Greater Mind of the Absolute.

Man is physically part of the vast structure of organic life which is directed and sustained by a cosmic intelligence. This has laid down programmes of response to stimuli appropriate to the many different forms of life, programmes which have evolved with astounding ingenuity; and the physical body is subject to a similar cosmic direction. But man is a special creation provided in addition with an individual mind which, despite his illusions of grandeur he uses very indifferently. In fact, in his customary state of (psychological) sleep he makes little or no use of his real possibilities but is governed almost entirely by impersonal cosmic influences. It is said that if these were properly understood they would be beneficial but in practice they are wrongly interpreted and result in inhumanity and violence.

What is the function of this individual mind of which we are so little aware? Briefly, it is provided to permit the development of *conscious* responses to the events of life. But this has to be done in stages. When Essence first occupies a body at birth its immediate requirement is the establishment of a satisfactory working relationship with the strange new environment. Its awareness of the world is derived from the constant stream of impressions received by the senses; but these isolated bits of information have no personal significance unless they can be related to some meaningful pattern. Hence the first duty of the mind is to lay down programmes of *meaning,* in obedience to which the brain will begin to co-ordinate the random influx of information by recognising similarity and purpose. This creates what we call associations which grow in number with experience and are all stored in the elaborate network of memory which determines all subsequent behaviour.

Yet there are different qualities of meaning. For example, a flower will convey a meaning quite different from an income-tax demand or a game of football. Hence associations fall into separate categories depending upon the functions with which they are primarily concerned. Some are instinctive while others deal with the voluntary activities of the body such as movement, feeling and thinking, each of which involves its own pattern of associations. Gurdjieff called these sub-divisions 'Centres', which should work in harmony but in practice rarely do.

The concept of Centres reconciles the conventional idea of the mind with the more significant interpretation as an intelligence in the unmanifest realm. The Centres are intelligences, but of a mechanical quality, being composite programmes of behaviour developed in the brain by the direction of the superior intelligence of the real mind; and since this can operate at different levels, the associations which the brain creates can also be of differing quality. For example, the exercise of creative thought and discovery involves associations of incomparably greater quality than those required in aimless chatter.

Hence each Centre can operate at several levels according to the level of the mind which is directing it at the time. The lowest or external levels are concerned with the mechanical associations necessary for the everyday conduct of life. With these we are content for a long time, and allow them to operate with no further direction so that our behaviour becomes automatic and full of inconsistencies and confusions. However, if we can arouse ourselves from our habitual slumber, the mind can lay down programmes of a different order which permit more conscious interpretations of events; and this creates associations of a higher quality operating in the inner parts of Centres.

It is evident that the Centres are of considerable importance in our lives. They are in fact the arbiters of behaviour since all our reactions are derived from almost instantaneous reference by the brain to the established patterns of associations. So that although we believe that we have freedom of thought and action our behaviour is entirely conditioned by programmes in the appropriate Centre. If we are content with the stereotyped programmes of habit – which is a comfortable existence – we have no real freedom; but the possibility exists of creating more significant programmes if we are prepared to make the effort.

There are five Centres which control our ordinary behaviour, one cosmic and four individual. The first is the Instinctive Centre which is concerned with the maintenance of the bodily functions such as breathing, circulation of the blood, digestion of food and nourishment of the tissues including the nervous system and the brain. These are all involuntary activities which the body performs automatically. They are not directed by individual consciousness but are responses to programmes laid down by a part of the impersonal intelligence of organic life which comes into play at the moment of conception and continues to operate throughout the life. It is evidently a very clever intelligence which should be acknowledged with a sense of wonder.

There are then three further Centres which are concerned with the voluntary activities of movement, emotion and thought. These are said to be blank at birth, meaning that they do not contain any ready-made programmes but have to be populated by experience, and to this extent they are individual.

Moving Centre, for example, is concerned with the movements of the body, for which we believe that we are personally responsible. Actually all these movements are responses to programmes which have had to be learned by trial and error. Initially a small amount of conscious direction is required but once the technique has been acquired the relevant associations are established and thereafter operate automatically, as for instance in riding a bicycle – a skill which once acquired is never forgotten. Throughout the day the body makes innumerable movements which we take entirely for granted, all directed by the intelligence of Moving Centre. We ought to be more appreciative of the speed and efficiency with which it reacts to our (mostly unconscious) desires.

One extraordinary programme which has always intrigued me is that which keeps our feet on the ground. The eyes, which are really small cameras, focus the image of the scene on the retina *upside down.* Hence to touch the ground the initial reaction is to raise the arm. The brain finds by experience that this is the wrong way round, and inverts its interpretation of the image, so that thereafter all our movements are properly oriented.

One might expect this to be instinctive, but if we observe a small baby it can be seen learning this inversion by experiment, making the wrong movements until it establishes the necessary associations in its Moving Centre. The inversion, in fact, is an acquired faculty, as was confirmed by an experiment in which a man was fitted with some special glasses which focused the image on the retina the right way up. This completely confused the brain, but after a few days of trial and error it learned to change its programme and the man was able to behave quite normally, even to the extent of playing tennis, or riding a bicycle.

Psychological activities require a different kind of programme. Thinking, for example, is directed by the Intellectual Centre which is concerned with comparisons. It assembles the information provided by the senses and compares one item with another in order to form an opinion. This is the process of reasoning which is the basis of ordinary knowledge. By its very nature it depends upon choice between opposites, often called Yes-or-No thinking, which is satisfactory and even necessary for life situations. However, it is possible for the intellectual mind to create more imaginative associations which are not circumscribed by conventional logic but can embrace both the opposites, and this can lead to new dimensions of understanding.

This wider thinking can be assisted by co-operation with the intelligence of Emotional Centre. This we are liable to misunderstand because emotion is customarily defined as 'agitation of mind' which implies an unbalanced and undesirable state. The Emotional Centre, however, is concerned with awareness of harmony and truth. This finds expression in the appreciation of beauty but more significantly in the recognition of connections and relationships beyond the perceptions of the ordinary senses. We have all experienced the occasional flash of intuition which conveys a feeling of rightness in a situation or perhaps provides a solution to a problem which has puzzled us for days, or even longer. The classic example is the inspiration of the mathematician Sir William Hamilton, who suddenly perceived, while walking over a bridge in Dublin, the hitherto unknown concept of vector algebra.

Emotions are not the same as feelings which are mostly mechanical expressions of like or dislike derived from instinctive sensations. These are quite genuine in themselves but by a wrong use of Emotional Centre we interpret them personally, introducing elements of criticism and resentment. What should be a simple reaction is adulterated by the desires and judgments of the False Personality, creating a whole range of 'negative emotions' which have no right to exist and only sap our energy.

Emotional Centre is really the most valuable of the tools at our disposal because it is programmed by a level of the mind which can recognise the relationships in the real (unmanifest) world. It can see *as a whole* the patterns from which the transit of time creates the successive events of life. It can be aware objectively of all the activities of the body, both physical and psychological, and can see their place and use. Most important of all, it can create conscious associations through which we can begin to make contact with inestimably higher levels of intelligence in the Universe which Gurdjieff called Higher Centres. But in practice we misuse this remarkable Centre for the gratification of personal desires which is not only wasteful but can be very dangerous.

There is a fifth intelligence called Sex Centre which is even more misunderstood, because sex is so often associated with lasciviousness. Actually it is directed by a higher level of mind than the other Centres, concerned with the integration of opposing principles. This is the basis of real growth, as one sees in Nature by the conjunction of male and female elements. Part of the function of Sex Centre is the direction of physical attraction and consummation but its more important aspects are psychological. One of its concerns is the transformation of the negative emotions just mentioned into useful material for the creation of the Astral body.

It is said that the role of the Sex Centre is to create an equilibrium among the other Centres which should be subordinate to its direction; but in the absence of a conscious control its high-quality energy is stolen by the lower Centres which then work with undue fervour. Intellectual activities become fanatical, always disputing, criticising and advancing disruptive theories. The Emotional Centre preaches hell and damnation, works up revolutions, kills and burns in the name of God; while Moving Centre indulges in frenzied competition, excessive tension and/or exaggerated gestures. All this useless activity results from the use by the ordinary Centres of too high a quality of energy for which they are not designed, which prevents them from performing their proper functions.

The idea of conscious control is important. We can appreciate that the Centres are intelligences which direct the various activities of the body but we do not realise that they themselves are subject to direction, which is, or should be, exercised by the higher level of intelligence called the mind. It is important to recognise that the mind, by its very nature, is not just an extension of ordinary awareness but is an intelligence of a different order having a perceptiveness and understanding appertaining to the higher-dimensional realms of the spirit.

It is part of the intelligence-material which permeates the whole Universe and so is impersonal in character. However, Essence receives a certain individual allocation when it comes down to Earth to enable it to use and transform the experiences of life in the fulfilment of its purpose. As said earlier, its first task is the establishment of a working relationship to the new environment in which it finds itself. For this it uses the lowest or formatory level of the available intelligence to create the necessary life associations; and since these prove to be practical and apparently completely satisfactory, it is inclined to rest content and relinquish any conscious control.

As a result everything happens at random. The wrong Centres are allowed to direct operations. We act when we should think. We think when we should feel. In a fit of pique we allow Emotional Centre to drive the car, which it does very badly and often disastrously. The 'we' concerned, of course, is the mechanical person of the day, not consciously directed by the real self which has gone to sleep.

But if Essence arouses itself and listens to the conscious influences from higher places it can begin to use the deeper levels of the mind which can create associations of a superior quality; and these will produce interpretations of events so different from the ordinary as to create new possibilities of understanding. For one thing, they operate in an entirely different time scale so that their operation is not only quicker but wider in scope. Instead of receiving only one impression of a situation one is now aware of thousands.

Actually not only the parts of Centres but the Centres them-selves work with different speeds determined by the quality of energy which they use, but this will be better discussed in another talk. The important requirement is to recognise the existence of this unmanifest mind with which Essence has been endowed and to try to make practical use of its potentialities.

6

Growth of Essence

It has been said that the whole object of the sojourn on earth is to promote the growth of Essence, i.e. the real part of us as distinct from the Personality, which is artificial. To some extent we understand this, realising that our behaviour is that of a machine which is not really ourselves but is being used to contend with the requirements of life. But though this is good and practical psychology our ideas of Essence are apt to remain rather vague.

So what do we understand by Essence? It is a spiritual entity, living in the body, so that it is of a different quality from the Personality. It can be regarded as a remote outpost of Heaven which has no interest in me – the 'me' of which I am ordinarily aware and with which I am completely identified.

We think of Essence as something which belongs to us. I think this is the wrong way round and that it is we who belong to Essence, which is using the body for its spiritual needs. It has come down, we are told, from a very high level of the Universe. We sometimes say that it has come down to Earth, but this is incorrect. It comes down to the level of the Astral world, World 24, at which point it is given a body which it can use as a tool in order to explore World 48, the phenomenal world. So you see that Essence is not part of Earth, but only visiting it.

What is the purpose of this visit? Basically, it is a search for food. Essence, like a small child, needs nourishment if it is to grow, and uses the body as a mechanism through which it can look out at the external world through the windows of the senses to prospect for suitable material.

However, in its natural state this material is not of a suitable quality. It is like the ore of the geologist which is a useful raw material but has to be refined if it is to yield the precious metal it contains. Similarly, psychological ore, which exists in profusion at the level of Earth, has to be refined so that it can yield a material on which Essence can feed.

What does this involve in practice? Quite simply (though by no means easily) it involves the conscious interpretation of the events of life. How do we know what is going on in the world around us? As you know, this is the result of interpretations by the brain of incoming impressions through the use of a whole host of associations. These we develop from our very earliest childhood. We are instructed by our parents and our teachers in the requirements of life, and augment this by experience until we build up a vast library of associations to which the brain refers in order to interpret the constant influx of information supplied by the senses.

Most of these associations are used entirely unconsciously. A given situation always produces the same kind of reaction and for certain purposes in life it is just as well that it does, because we do not want to have to think what to do to get out of the way of a motor car. So these associations have their use but only to a limited extent. If there is to be any real use of the available faculties we have to begin to cultivate associations of a different quality, associations that are related to the idea of a Universe of levels, the idea of the existence of higher intelligences.

The first such level is the level of World 24, the Astral world, in which Essence lives and of which material it is itself composed. The very recognition of the existence of this level will awaken the deeper levels of the mind which can begin to create and use associations of a superior kind, so that one can occasionally

37

translate an event in terms other than one's own self-love; and these new associations will begin to transform the events of life. They will not transform the happening. The physical event will remain the same, but the way we take it can be changed out of all recognition, and you can understand that to the extent that this is done the quality of the experience is raised and it becomes suitable food for Essence.

This is conscious participation in events, which involves the recognition of the existence of this spiritual entity within us which is crying out for food. We must begin to feel the presence of this spirit, not as an intellectual possibility but as an actuality – the only real thing we possess, which has come down from the high level of its origin for the express purpose of climbing back to its real home; but to do this it has to grow, and to grow it needs food.

Once we begin to realise the absolute necessity of providing this nourishment our outlook changes completely. For one thing, we see that it is necessary to develop a strong and rich Personality because the more experiences we have in life, the more life knowledge we possess, the more ability, the more skill, the greater the opportunities they present. They provide an increased supply of raw material, which is excellent as long as we realise that it is to be worked on and used. So we can enjoy our life experiences as long as we remember ourselves.

We begin to feel what it is that Essence really needs, what it is we really want from life. Events are no longer regarded as an end in themselves but as experiences which can be savoured; and this has a most valuable corollary since in this condition there cannot be any sense of guilt. We constantly wallow in feelings of guilt, of regret, of remorse which are not only useless but contaminate the ore which we are so patiently extracting. If we can see that every experience is a gift, every day is a gift, and that everything that happens can be used, there is no longer any feeling of guilt, only a feeling of hunger; and this can be very acute.

Nicoll says in one of his Commentaries that if Essence does not grow it will attract the same situations in recurrence. The idea is sometimes expressed by saying that one's being attracts one's life. Perhaps you do not see that what happens to you is determined by Essence. One's life is not a succession of chance manifestations, but conforms to an already established pattern. At first we find this an unpalatable idea. It savours of a gloomy predestination, but this is a wrong interpretation.

It is true that as long as one is content to use the stereotyped interpretations of habit, the pattern of the life is determined. Indeed we use this fact in dealing with other people. Their behaviour is predictable and if we want something from them we choose our approach accordingly. (It does not usually occur to us that we are equally predictable.)

A deeper level of the mind will see a different and more significant interpretation. If one can accept the idea that Essence is in some way responsible for the pattern of one's life there may be a reason for it. There is the well-known idea, expressed by Maeterlink in *The Blue Bird* and centuries earlier by Plato in the Myth of Er, that we have chosen our life. The choice is not made by the Personality but by the superior intelligence of the soul which will know what kinds of event can provide the greatest opportunities for its own development.

Essence is of the material of Astral world, which is a timeless realm in which there exist patterns of possibilities which are the causes of the events of life. It contains innumerable threads interwoven into the fabric, produced by transits of consciousness which bring into being the events and situations in the phenomenal world. My Essence will be responsible for the thread which determines my life, but if it is undeveloped and ill-nourished it will not have the ability to make any change in the situation. Yet it is aware of the whole pattern, from birth to death, and if it grows in stature it can modify the path through the eternal fabric to create events which will provide it with better food.

This is the idea of recurrence. Since the life, with all its experiences, is brought into being by a transit of consciousness through the pattern existing in the Astral world, it is clearly possible for this transit to be repeated. If it is repeated exactly we shall be born of the same parents in the same circumstances and experience the same situations until we die from the same cause. But there is the possibility of other transits, which will actualise different possibilities; but this we interpret in a complacent hope that perhaps 'next time' may be better. This is mere imagination born of our · perpetual hankering for a second chance.

We have to learn to use the existing situation, because until we do so it must be repeated. The life is a pattern of opportunities which the soul has prescribed in its quest for nourishment. But the greatest error in our conventional interpretation of recurrence is the assumption that the transits of consciousness must be consecutive. They can be modified – and can only be modified – now.

So you can see emotionally, without the distraction of reasoning, that a developing Essence can create a different path through the pattern and so attract different events; and this can alter the situation now. I do not have to wait for death and a mythical next time. Yet this can only start by providing Essence with the food it needs by transforming the experiences of the day. These constitute the 'ore' which can only be found at this level of Earth; and this is why we are down here.

7

Memory and Time-Body

We live in a world which is entirely conditioned by passing time. It is a structure in which information can only be conveyed by changes of condition. The physical senses are mechanisms of response to change. For example, the sounds we hear are caused by small variations in air pressure which the ears detect and the brain interprets accordingly. In absolutely still air we hear nothing, and the other senses are similarly time-dependent.

We are not conscious of this as such, but only of the effects. Our awareness of situations, in fact, is derived from interpretations resulting from the associations we have acquired through experience. In the process we discover that events follow one another in an apparently inexorable transit from past to future which we accept as an inevitable condition of existence beyond our control.

This is illusion. The body is certainly in the bondage of time, but the spirit is not. The sense of time is an acquired faculty resulting from associations laid down by experience in the various Centres of the brain. It is part of what is called our first education, the development of expertise in contending with the everyday conditions of life, in the course of which we build up an enormous pattern of associations called memory.

Memory is another of the activities which we take for granted. The very fact that we are able to remember previous experiences

41

is a remarkable ability, without which we could not survive. For instance, the simple operation of walking, to which we never give a thought, involves the almost instant memory of a sequence of operations learned by trial and error in childhood. All our behaviour, in fact, is dependent on memory.

What is the mechanism of this extraordinary faculty? It used to be thought that every experience was stored in the brain, available for recall when required, but this is obviously incorrect because it would simply result in an enormous and increasing collection of clutter, which the brain could not possibly accommodate.

The directing intelligence which we call the mind makes a more intelligent use of the facilities by relating memory to *meaning*. We only remember facts or situations which have significance, or to which we have given attention. The brain, we are told, is a vast network of small elements called neurones. These behave like simple electrical 'gates' which pass on nerve impulses if certain conditions are complied with, determined by previously established associations. There is thus literally a train of thought culminating in appropriate action, after which each neurone reverts to normal, ready for further impulses. Hence the neurones are not permanently activated, but any subsequent impression which has the same quality of meaning will reactivate the same sequence and the brain 'remembers'. Hence it is associations which are stored in the brain – actually in the appropriate parts of the Centres – and not the incidents.

It is clear that memory can exist in several Centres. Take, for example, memories of a visit to Paris. Instinctive Centre has memory of the food and the comfortable beds. Emotional Centre perhaps has memory of the beauty of the sunrise over the Seine. Intellectual Centre may have memory of the symbolism of Notre Dame. Moving Centre has memory of the need to get out of the way of the traffic! So you have four different memories, and memory in all Centres is much more vivid than casual memory in just one Centre.

Memory and Time-Body

Memory, however, can be very fallible. If the associations on which it is based are purely objective it is usually both efficient and reliable. It tells us, for example, which way to go when walking home. We can remember without effort our multiplication tables or even quite complicated items of scientific knowledge. But if the memories are subjective, as in the recollection of incidents in the past in which we have been involved, the association patterns become adulterated by the demands of False Personality such as self-esteem or resentment, so that we 'remember' the incident in the most favourable light. We reject, quite unconsciously, the true recollection and substitute a modified version more to our liking, and are convinced that this imaginary version is completely accurate. Subjective memory, in fact, is hardly ever true.

Now, while objective memory is necessary in the conduct of life the value of the subjective memory is questionable. We recognise people by a virtually unconscious use of memory but this has been coloured from the very first moment of meeting by opinions of liking or disliking, later reinforced by judgments and criticisms. So we never see the person but only the image created by our attitudes. The same applies even more pertinently to the events of the day which we never interpret objectively but always by an equally unconscious reference to the memory of previous experience.

Hence, although we do not realise it, we normally live entirely in the past, accompanied by an imaginative expectancy of the future based on the same stereotyped memory. We do not even use this memory intelligently. If we did, we might understand that progress in time occurs in cycles with alternating periods of good and bad fortune. We might begin to live in the present, to accept the events of the day without judgment, recognising that they are exactly what we need, and have in fact asked for.

This would be the beginning of freedom – of freedom from the bondage of conventional time. The body, with its senses and interpretive mechanisms, is necessarily subject to the laws of passing time. Yet this body is only a vehicle designed to be used by Essence, which is not subject to these laws but belongs to and operates in a superior realm in which time is not transient.

Within this realm there can be a different kind of memory which is not a recollection of events but an awareness of the whole of one's experience. Swedenborg called this the interior memory, as distinct from the exterior memory of the senses, which he said contained a permanent record of the life. But actually this record is of an entirely different quality, concerned with the pattern of the life in the unmanifest world.

This is for us the real world, usually called the Astral world. It is a realm directed by the intelligence of World 24 which is of a superior order. In particular, it has a different time-scale so that for us everything in it exists eternally. Eternity is usually interpreted as implying endless repetition, an infinite extension of the present, but it is better understood to mean continually existing.

It is the realm containing the unseen patterns which control the behaviour of the visible world. It is evidently not material in the conventional sense but can be envisaged as a kind of fabric of possibilities – not events – through which certain lines or tracks have been laid down by the Astral intelligence. One can think of these as lines drawn by a celestial artist on this fabric, lines which one would surmise are not only meaningful but form wonderful and elaborate patterns, as an actual artist would do on a piece of canvas. The Astral intelligence then arranges that the possibilities on the various tracks are actualised in sequence by the operation of passing time, and this produces the events of life which we know from experience follow in succession. They are the implementation or actualisation of the possibilities in one or other of the many different tracks.

Now, the total span of any given track is called the time-body of the object concerned. In the case of a man or woman it will commence at a certain point in the Astral fabric (which includes the whole of time), will pass through the innumerable possibilities which become manifest as the events of the life and will end at some later point of time when the person dies.

There are many, many time-bodies in the Astral realm, which contains the time-body of every object and event in the phenomenal world. The earth itself has its time-body, as also do the denizens of organic life which cover its surface. All of these intersect at appropriate points, each having its own life time. The whole phenomenal world is the manifestation of a vast structure of interconnected time-bodies in the unmanifest world, generated by transits in passing time through the already appointed tracks in the eternal fabric, transits which occur mechanically and without deviation by the direction of the overall intelligence of the Astral realm in accordance with the cosmic plan.

Man, however, is a special creation provided with an individual allocation of Astral intelligence which we call Essence, which can create an independent track through the eternal fabric, and this is capable of variation if the events of life are interpreted by the deeper, more conscious levels of the mind. However, if he is content to use only the formatory mind his life pursues its allotted course mechanically. Despite his illusions of free will, everything happens in the only way it can and he is no more than a unit in the cosmos of earth.

The deeper levels of the mind are intelligences of Astral quality and can thus be aware of the pattern as a whole and will recognise the path which Essence has created. This will be interior memory – memory in Essence, which is completely objective. But clearly this cannot be brought into play by the conventional mind, but only by the deeper, more conscious levels; and by the very fact that it is a conscious exercise it will begin to nourish Essence, which in turn can begin to modify the path through the pattern.

Evidently the awakening of real memory is important. The first step is to begin to feel the existence of one's time-body, which embraces the whole of the life. All the experiences of the so-called past, the successes and failures, the delights and disappointments, are present in the Astral pattern. Good relationships established in an earlier period still exist in the time-body, even though the person concerned may no longer be physically present. Even the stupidities and inadequacies, or maybe antagonisms, which ordinary memory recalls with such distaste, can be re-examined and interpreted more consciously, in which case *the past is changed*. This is a significant idea which we do not understand at first; but an event is far more than the physical happening. It includes all the psychological reactions of the people concerned and we can change our own interpretations without altering the physical happening. Indeed, we may not want to, because the value of any event is determined entirely by the use which we make of it.

Astral consciousness is aware of the whole of the life from birth to death simultaneously (which would of course include the future). This level of understanding is normally beyond us, but we can begin to see incidents in the life as parts of a coherent whole and in so doing can recognise events as opportunities. We can see where the course of time has been, or is, leading us into sterile regions and try to modify the route to provide more significant possibilities.

However, this requires the use of a higher order of consciousness which will know what variations in the path are permissible in order to fulfil the purpose of our existence. Each one of us is pursuing his or her life for the purpose of serving the higher levels of the Universe, serving God if you prefer it, and therefore any change in the time-body can only be directed by a level of consciousness which is aware of the reason for the sojourn on earth. You can see that this is utterly different from trying to change one's life to make it more comfortable. This is not the sort of change which is permitted. You can change the past, you can change the time-body, *only* for the glory of God, otherwise it is imagination.

One of the aids to self-remembering suggested by Gurdjieff

was the occasional repetition of the phrase 'I wish to be'. But how do we interpret this? Do we not think of it in terms of becoming – something to be attained in the future? To wish to be can only mean to wish to be aware of *what is,* without contriving of any kind, and this is by no means an easy task. By means of the concept of time-body we can begin to envisage what is meant by being. It means being present – present in the eternal pattern which has been laid down for me to pursue – a pattern known to my real self, but with which I have lost touch and so have forgotten my aim; but I can begin to accept the idea that my life has been laid down specifically to provide opportunities.

This is no doctrine of predestination. The pattern which has been laid down contains the possibility of change by conscious attention and this is the meaning of life. Do you see how this enriches one's whole understanding? There are so many aspects of this idea that are luminous in the extreme. One of them is that we do not exist in isolation. Our time-bodies are continually intersecting those of other people, an idea which has enormous implications. It means, for one thing, that what I do affects you. I cannot live in myself alone, like a neat little parcel. As John Donne said, 'No man is an island'. We are each involved with the time-bodies of everyone else with whom we are or have been in contact; which is an enormous idea.

Real memory exists in Essence, which is eternal; and some of the innate tendencies with which we are born are created by memories in Essence acquired during previous lives. Hence again there is a responsibility in the present life to be more conscious in our behaviour so that our time-body may contain material useful to Essence.

8

Essence and the Higher Bodies

We all have an intuitive feeling that the physical body is not the whole of ourselves but is merely the outward and visible part of a much larger spiritual entity which is not manifest to the senses. Yet because it is unmanifest this spiritual part has a somewhat abstract quality. Actually it is quite real, though not fully organised, and we should feel its presence much more than we do.

We are told that in addition to the physical body, which we are given at birth, man has the possibility of developing three further bodies, of progressively finer material, which will interpenetrate the coarse texture of the ordinary body. This is not difficult to understand when one realises that the apparently solid flesh is really a structure of microscopically small atoms separated by relatively enormous distances. This diffuse pattern can obviously be penetrated by finer substances so that we can regard the physical body as impregnated by materials of a lighter quality somewhat like a sponge which can hold within its pores liquids and gases, all within its containing shape.

Obviously this finer material, such as it is, is something belonging to the unmanifest world, that much greater part of the Universe which is not perceived by the senses; and we have seen that this realm is itself a structure of levels – a hierarchy of world-orders represented by the Ray of Creation discussed earlier. Each of these world-orders has its own intelligence and materiality, of descending scale, but they should not be regarded as separate because they are all part of a living whole in which every level is permeated by the materials of all the higher levels. So you will see that the body, which belongs to the physical world, nevertheless contains within its structure materials of spiritual quality.

It is in this sense that one can regard the body as a habitation for the spiritual entity conventionally called the soul. This, we are told, comes down from a very high level of the Universe. However, for cosmic reasons it is not created complete but has to develop by its own efforts, for which purpose it has to descend to the level of Earth in order to find suitable food. It is like a baby which has first to be fed on pap, but as it grows it is able to eat food of a higher quality.

So we must think of the real part of ourselves, which we have called Essence, as originating from the level of the Galaxy, World 6 in the Ray of Creation, which in Christian terminology is called the Divine level. It then passes through the Solar level, World 12, to the Astral level, World 24. This is the timeless realm containing the underlying patterns of the phenomenal world, and it is of this material that Essence is composed.

However, Essence is then required to climb back to the country of its origin, to do which it requires nourishment. It is therefore supplied with a physical body through which it can explore the territory of the phenomenal world and extract from it certain energies which can provide the food it needs.

Clearly the first task of Essence is to use the facilities of this physical body to establish a working relationship with the strange conditions of Earth. It therefore organises an intelligence or mind to direct the formation of appropriate patterns of associations. These enable the brain to interpret the information supplied by the senses so that the body is able to conduct itself competently in the world. This is the formation of the Personality which has to be well developed if it is to be a suitable source of food. However, these activities are exciting, so that this first adventure comes to be regarded as the whole requirement. Essence makes no further effort and, in effect, goes to sleep. This is the state of psychological sleep so often spoken of in the Gospels and it is to re-awaken Essence that esoteric teaching exists.

In this state of sleep there is no conscious control of the behaviour. There are two aspects of the body, namely its physical mechanisms and its psychological activities; but while the

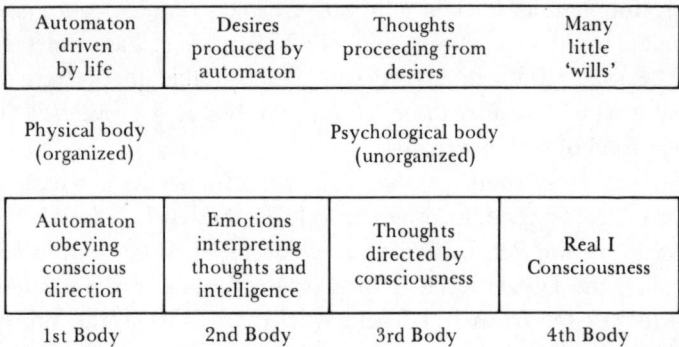

Automaton driven by life	Desires produced by automaton	Thoughts proceeding from desires	Many little 'wills'

| Physical body (organized) | | Psychological body (unorganized) | |

Automaton obeying conscious direction	Emotions interpreting thoughts and intelligence	Thoughts directed by consciousness	Real I Consciousness
1st Body	2nd Body	3rd Body	4th Body

Figure 2

physical part is very well organised the psychological part is virtually uncontrolled. The functions of feeling, thought and action are entirely determined by the random impact of life events. The situation can be illustrated diagrammatically as in Fig. 2.

Impressions from the environment are received by the senses and interpreted by the automatic use of habitual associations – by what is, in fact, an automaton. This leads to the almost instantaneous expression of feelings and desires from which develop thoughts culminating in a variety of small wills and intentions, few of which are consistent. The whole machinery, in fact, is driven from the wrong end, and the thoughts and feelings which we believe to be conscious are simply responses to the haphazard impressions of life.

Compare this with the situation if the psychology were organised. There would be a coherent direction by an objective consciousness which would be aware of the body as a tool to be used. It would create genuine thoughts and emotions, and instruct the automaton to produce meaningful actions. The same mechanism would be used but it would now be subject to conscious direction.

We are inclined to think of psychological activity as vaguely abstract, but actually it is basically physical. Feelings and thoughts are created by the brain in response to the established associative patterns and so are merely operations of the physical mechanism. But in the customary state of sleep the brain no longer receives any conscious direction so that its reactions are entirely automatic.

However, if the mind is awakened it can provide new programmes for the brain which will then create different ranges of thought and emotion relating to more real levels of the Universe; and these again can be of differing quality because the mind can operate at different levels. Hence, although the psychological reactions are still produced by the physical body they will be directed by a coherent intelligence.

What then awakens the appropriate mind and inspires its direction? It is the spiritual part of the man, operating at the level of what is called Real I, an intelligence of the quality of World 12 in the Ray of Creation. But this is not permanent in us. It may be briefly in control but can only be so for any length of time as a result of long and persistent effort. We have in us materials of Worlds 24, 12 and 6, though only in a vestigial form; but with appropriate effort it is possible to organise a concentration of the material of each of, these levels which acquires a certain permanency, and these constitute the higher bodies which can be created in us.

Now, while we can appreciate that if these higher bodies were formed and in control of our behaviour, we should experience an almost unimaginable increase in understanding, the important question is how they can be created in practice; because unlike the first body, which is given to us at birth, they do not exist as of right but have to be assembled by long and arduous individual effort. The materials are there. We have to find out how to organise them.

The first step is to recognise that Essence needs nourishment. This is the reason for its presence in the body, which has been provided for the specific purpose of exploring the phenomenal world in search of suitable food. However, this material is like ore, which can be extracted from the earth but has to be refined before it can be of practical use. Similarly the experiences of life have in some way to be refined before they can serve the requirements of Essence.

It is with this refinement that esoteric teaching is concerned; and it is basically very simple. It involves the conscious participation in the events of the day. We have of necessity to manipulate the situations of life to practical advantage; yet this begins to be accompanied by an expanded awareness which is not exclusively concerned with personal desires. We become conscious of the objects around us – including other people – as living beings contributing to the drama of existence; and we find unexpectedly that there is time to take in a vast number of impressions which are normally not noticed.

This, of course, does not just happen. It requires a conscious effort to make room for the interpretations of the deeper levels of the mind instead of allowing all our attention to dwell in the affairs of life, which are quite adequately handled by the established Personality. If this is done it is clear that the quality of the experience is transformed. The raw material of events has been refined to a condition in which it can provide the nourishment which Essence is seeking.

So this is the task. It involves the gradual creation of new qualities of associations, new programmes whereby the brain translates the same experiences much more vividly; and if the effort is maintained these more significant programmes become established and begin to operate automatically. This is the formation of a second, or Astral body, which now exercises some control over our behaviour, and maintains an increasing supply of refined material for the growth of Essence.

Second body is concerned with emotional perception and the programmes of Emotional Centre. Since it operates within the Astral realm it is aware of the underlying patterns of the events of life, which it sees as a whole, and hence understands the relationships which exist between the apparently isolated situations of earthly experience. The programmes which it provides for the Emotional Centre contain a similar understanding so that when this Centre is working properly it is able to see at a glance connections which logical reasoning can only arrive at very laboriously, if at all.

This second, or Astral body is not an abstract entity. It has a quite real existence, if it is formed, being composed of psychological materials already existing in us, but normally unorganised; and as such it can actually be seen if the emotional faculties are adequately developed. So that it is possible to see people as they really are – if there is anything real to be seen! I once wrote a story about an apprentice angel who was told to look after a group of people; but he returned to report in some dismay that he could not see them. Have we anything real within us which could be seen by angels?

It is sometimes said that the presence of Astral body can be detected as an aura round the ordinary body, but I think this is incorrect. Auras certainly exist, but they are manifestations of vital energy which is a concomitant of the physical body, and may be quite strong in a person or organism in which no higher bodies have been developed. Second body has to be created by individual effort. It does not exist automatically.

However, if this effort is sustained, the establishment of a second body will enable Essence to explore the Astral territory and begin to assemble associations of a still higher order, of the quality of the Solar level, World 12 in the Ray of Creation (see Fig. 3). This will lead to a transformation of Essence which will grow in stature to the level of Real I. This normally exists only vestigially, but if it can be nourished it can begin to exercise significant control of our actions and our understanding.

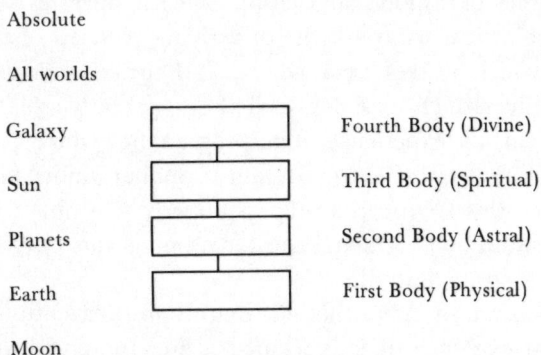

Absolute

All worlds

Galaxy		Fourth Body (Divine)
Sun		Third Body (Spiritual)
Planets		Second Body (Astral)
Earth		First Body (Physical)

Moon

Figure 3

The crystallisation of these superior associations begins to create third body, composed of material of the Solar level in which Real I can now grow. This is the realm of ideas, using the word idea in its true sense of archetype, the primary expression of the requirements of the Divine level, from which are created the wide range of inter-related patterns in the Astral world. Hence third body has to do with objective and creative thought, and the proper use of the intellectual mind; for which reason it is sometimes called Mental Body.

By a similar process the refinement of the Solar material can produce a fourth body, concerned with the exercise of consciousness and will. This will operate within the Divine level of World

6, which is the birthplace of the soul, so that attainment of this state is the perfection of the life. But this must not be envisaged with the time-conditioned logic of the senses. The effort to organise the higher bodies can be made at several levels at different times, sometimes simultaneously. Hence they can be regarded as co-existing in the timeless realms of eternity and may be inhabited briefly by the soul at any moment.

9

Imaginary I

Humanity suffers from a pernicious disease called 'internal considering', a disease which is the more debilitating because it is unsuspected; and it is brought about by the activities of a still less recognised person called 'Imaginary I'.

We labour under the delusion that our behaviour is controlled by an intelligent self bearing our name, which we call I; but actually this self is very rarely present, because our everyday reactions are dependent on patterns of associations, established by experience, to which the brain refers automatically. Every event calls into play a small group of appropriate associations which determine the response, so that our behaviour is really controlled by a succession of automata.

This is an effective way of contending with life. It enables the brain to make instant decisions without laborious calculation, and without having to refer to us. Indeed so little are we aware of the situation that we identify ourselves with these automata, saying I to each in turn, even though they are often neither intelligent nor consistent.

Some of the acquired associations are objective, concerned with the acquisition of knowledge and skills in life. They form the basis of the Personality. But there are many more which are purely subjective, concerned only with an entirely imaginary self which we have been brought up from a very early age to regard as of paramount importance; and these are not only useless but a great hindrance.

The illusion of this precious imaginary self, this imaginary I, creates a whole host of spurious associations from which is built up an entirely fictitious False Personality. If we could see it, it would be amusing, but because we are so blind it has a devastating effect on our behaviour. We become obsessed by a whole host of unnecessary and useless requirements. We are concerned with what other people think of us. Strictly speaking it is only this false self which is so concerned, but we are not intelligent enough to see it in those terms. It would be much better if we did. But I continually wonder what people think of me, whether I have behaved rightly, have behaved honourably. Do people really appreciate me? Do they treat me with the respect which is due to me, because after all I have some knowledge and experience and I expect to be treated accordingly. So I resent it if I do not receive this acclamation. I may not express this outwardly but I shall still resent it inside. When a somewhat illiterate shop assistant calls me 'Ducks' I resent it.

This is the False Personality at work and it leads one constantly to judge other people and events. We judge them entirely in relation to whether it is what I want, this quite imaginary thing called 'I'. We place the whole feeling of ourselves in this imaginary self and are completely identified with its behaviour. We start to make accounts against people. If someone does not behave in the way I want them to I hold it against them and if they continually fail to do what I want, the account becomes a very large one, so much so that I will avoid that particular person. I do not want to know them. (It does not occur to me that perhaps they find me equally objectionable.)

We make accounts against situations, sometimes of long ago, as for example having been punished in one's youth for something one had not done. We make accounts against the weather for raining when we had planned an excursion or for not raining when the plants are in so much need of moisture. We make accounts against Fate (though we do not say thankyou if things are going well).

We live, in fact, in a constant state of *internal considering*. To consider means to weigh up or assess information; but our assessments are almost always related to the demands of this imaginary self – this so important self which must be gratified. So we are never at peace.

We may perhaps observe some of the more obvious demands of False Personality, but nearly always with justification. After all, we say, one must stand up for oneself. Or we make excuses by saying it is just the machine, as if this absolved us of responsibility. Internal considering is a subtle disease which is constantly sapping our strength in unsuspected ways, one of which is what Nicoll calls 'singing one's songs'. There is a continual background of demands made by the False Personality which we put together in little songs and moans of disgruntlement. If only I had had better opportunities when I was younger. If only I had been able to go to a University. If only my parents had understood me better. If only, for that matter, other people could understand me better – because nobody really understands me, they do not realise what a very shy and retiring person I am and how bravely I put on a front.

This is a song. Whether you sing this particular song is for you to decide, but we all have our pet songs and we usually sing them when things begin to go wrong in life. When we run up against troubles of some kind or another, up comes a suitable song so that we wallow in our discomfort. There are other songs which are not so despondent, in fact rather the reverse. There is the song which says I am always reliable. If anybody asks me to do anything, I can be relied on to do it. There are songs which say – I am an honourable person and by and large I do not tell lies. You can find your own examples of typical songs, many of them more like hymns of praise. We have gradually to begin to see that they are quite false and often blatantly untrue;

so that perhaps we may sing them a little less vociferously, even possibly only occasionally.

This singing of songs is responsible for much of our relationship with other people becàuse we pick friends who respond to our particular song. What we do not always realise is that sometimes the other person begins to get a little tired of this song and may repulse us somewhat violently; and then of course fresh accounts start to be made and we look around for someone else on whom to inflict our songs.

These songs, and their accompanying inner talking, are mainly concerned with certain predominant aspects of the False Personality which Gurdjieff called Chief Feature. It is clearly an individual characteristic. For some it may be conceit, for others anxiety or fear. It may be greed or envy and many other things which we have to discover for ourselves, though this is not easy because we are not honest in our observations and thrust aside anything we do not like the look of. Other people can see it more easily and we can sometimes learn from them.

Chief Feature, however, should not be regarded with distaste. If we can begin to see it, without criticism or feeling of guilt, it can become the point of greatest opportunity, the place where our efforts to awaken can be most effective. Many years ago I wrote to Dr. Nicoll bemoaning some trouble. He replied, 'Why do you take everything with a sigh? I would rejoice – rejoice to know that if you can learn how to pay, by working on Chief Feature, you will be given things all your life'.

Note that he said working on, not working against. This seems to me to be a vital distinction. To work against any manifestation of the machine has an implication of guilt which destroys understanding. If I can learn how to use these manifestations there is a complete difference in approach. I am not my machine but am only inhabiting it. It is an extremely clever piece of equipment which has been specially provided to enable me to make use of the situations and events of life; and if this can be done, the energy which they contain can be transformed in quality and becomes of value to higher levels of the Universe.

Evidently there is here an entirely different approach, a change of attitude transcending the demands of the Imaginary I. It involves what is called *external considering*. This is something we do not understand for a long time. We imagine that it means to put oneself in the place of someone else – which might be useful if we could see them as they really are, and not through the distorting lens of False Personality. We might then be able to help them, but our attempts to help others are all too often mere internal considering, based on a feeling of superiority.

External considering is an impersonal exercise. It is based on relationship to the Universe, on a relationship to something which is not oneself. It involves the beginning of understanding of the place and purpose of everything in the Universe including oneself, the real self that one begins to see is a spirit inhabiting a body for a purpose. Obviously this purpose is utterly different from the gratification of personal desire, so we have gradually to ease that out of the picture and wait for a real appreciation to be given to us, which cannot happen as long as we are completely identified with the imaginary self.

But if one has begun to move in this direction various reversals take place. I am no longer concerned with what I am owed, with what is due to me. I begin to see that it is possible that I owe something myself. We ask in the familiar prayer which we repeat so perfunctorily that our 'trespasses' may be forgiven. But the original wording is much more significant. It says 'cancel our *debts,* as we cancel what (we think) is owed to us'. What do we owe – and to whom? How rarely do we offer any thanks for the situations which are given to us every day? I meet friends and acquaintances from whom I derive pleasure. Is it not marvellous that there should be this possibility of communication, that there should be all these people quite outside myself who are willing to talk to me? In the ordinary way I take it all for granted.

When one walks through life, what of all the wonderful

impressions that come in, the sights and sounds that surround one, the flowers, the trees, even the rainfall? It is said somewhere that this earth is the most beautiful planet in the Universe. Our ordinary attitudes regard it as an inimical planet, a planet full of difficulties, sometimes called the planet purgatory. This we misinterpret. These very difficulties make the earth a planet containing magnificent and continuing opportunities for the transformation of impressions; and that is why we are here.

Considering, we said, is a weighing up of information. Internal considering assesses everything in relation to an imaginary self. External considering is concerned with relationship to higher levels; and it is interesting that the very word 'considering' is derived from a Latin root meaning a star. Can you glimpse the magnificence of the feeling that we are part of the starry galaxy and have a joyous duty to try to behave in conformity with the plan for which we were created?

Round the meeting room in the Gurdjieff Institute at Fontainebleau was a series of aphorisms intended to remind people of their real purpose. One of these ran, 'The chief implement for living felicitously in life is the ability to consider externally always, internally never'. I recall a remark made by Dr Nicoll to some of us in his study, that the only thing that can provide meaning in life is to live according to the laws of a higher organism. This is the law of unselfishness, to live not for the individual but for the Divine whole.

10

Triads and Octaves

Although the events of life sometimes appear to be entirely haphazard, we are told that the Universe is essentially an ordered
structure. Certainly this is true of physical and chemical
behaviour which is determined by precise and elegant laws.
However, these are merely detailed applications of two fundamental laws which apply throughout the whole Universe, in
appropriate form at the successive levels.

The first of these is the Law of Three of which we saw the
application on macroscopic scale when discussing the devolution
of the world-orders (in Chapter 3). Science does not understand
this law but sees everything in terms of action and reaction,
which are said in the well-known axiom to be equal and
opposite. Yet this is clearly a condition from which nothing
can develop, a condition of stalemate. If anything is to happen
some additional force must come into play which can in some
way bring these opposing forces into a useful relationship.
So if there is to be any manifestation, any event or change of
state, *three* forces have to be involved. There is first an active
force, a desire or intention; but this automatically induces an
opposing or passive force which resists the intention, and unless
there is some third force which can make the desired result
possible nothing will happen. The third force, in fact, is often
called the enabling or neutralising force.

We are not accustomed to thinking in terms of forces. We

recognise perhaps that a magnet will exercise a force of attraction on a piece of iron, or that things fall to the ground as a result of the force of gravity, but in general we see the world as composed of objects and materials. However, the events of life are produced by interactions between materials, and these will depend upon the type of force which they are conducting at the time. Consider, for example, a windmill. The wind will conduct active force, exerting a pressure which the building will withstand by conducting passive force and there will be a state of equilibrium and no event; but if the mill is provided with sails which can turn they can conduct a third force so that the force of the wind can produce a useful result. Yet in the absence of any wind both the mill and the sails will be quiescent, conducting no force.

Every object or situation, in fact, may at a given time conduct any one of the three forces, or none of them. Nor are events necessarily entirely physical. If I want to pick up a stone from the ground my desire will conduct first force, while the stone, which a moment ago was quite neutral, will now conduct passive force. But there will be no result until my hand conducts the necessary relating force and actually grasps the stone; yet a moment later it may conduct active force by pitching the stone away. This is a trivial example, but our understanding of life is increased if we begin to recognise the involvement of three forces in every event. We may not see, at first, what the third force is but we can be aware of the other two, particularly in personal requirements. We can ask ourselves exactly what it is that we want. This will at once disclose the inevitable difficulties which will arise, and may indicate the kind of relating force necessary to make the aim possible. It will certainly involve some kind of effort, which all too often we are not prepared to make.

An arrangement of three forces in the right relationship is called a triad, and the Universe is a structure of numerous interconnected triads. In many of them the three forces are of similar quality, in which case the resultant is of the same character.

However, there are others in which the forces are of different levels, and these will produce a change of state or condition. The digestion of food in the body, for instance, involves a succession of triads by which the coarse material of physical food is transformed into the intangible energies of thought and feeling, while conversely there are creative triads through which ideas can be converted into practical form.

Any such progressive development, however, does not take place at random. It has to conform to a specific pattern determined by the second of the two fundamental laws – the Law of Seven, which controls the order of manifestation. This says that any effective progress can only be achieved in a succession of seven stages, culminating in a replica of the original state at a different level. The complete pattern thus forms a series of eight, which is called an octave.

The intervals between the stages, however, are not uniform but obey a curious pattern of hidden harmony which is conveniently represented by the successive notes of the major musical scale. To many people this is just one of the technicalities of music, an arrangement which just happens to be pleasing to the ear (though Asian and Eastern countries use an entirely different scale). Actually it is not a haphazard sequence but is based on harmony, and is said to have been devised by an ancient esoteric school to preserve the pattern for posterity. Now, a musical note is produced by regularly recurring vibrations in the air and the more rapid the vibration rate the higher is the pitch of the sound. In particular, if the rate of vibration is doubled the note has a similar tonal value but is higher in pitch, a replica of the original at a higher level.

The conventional musical scale is a progression from one note to its octave through seven intermediate notes. In musical language these notes are given the names Do, Re, Mi, Fa, Sol, La, Si, Do, in what is called the Tonic Sol-fa scale. (These names were actually chosen by a mediaeval monk, Guido d'Arezzo, from the initial letters of the hymn Sancte Iohannes, which is an interesting example of the use of words which can be repeated mechanically but are only understood by those who have the key.)

Note	Do	Re	Mi	Fa	Sol	La	Si	Do
Ratio of vibrations	1	9/8	5/4	4/3	3/2	5/3	15/8	2
Percentage increase	12.5	11.1	6.5	12.5	11.1	12.5	6.5	

Figure 4

However, if these notes are to have a harmonious relationship their vibration rates must be simple fractional multiples of the initial rate. The structure is illustrated in Fig. 4, and it will be seen that because of this pattern the intervals between the notes are not uniform. Five of them are roughly the same but in two places the interval is only half the normal, which is called musically a semitone. This may seem to be an arbitrary arrangement, but will be seen to be a consequence of the harmonic relationships between the notes. It is, in fact, an expression of the Law of Seven which requires that any developing process throughout the Universe must involve these two places of constriction where the development is impeded.

This is a most interesting natural law which is generally unrecognised. If progress is to be maintained it is necessary for some reinforcement to be provided at these points of shock as they are called; and in the absence of this shock the development will either stop or will take a wrong direction. The classic example of this is the Spanish Inquisition where an honest endeavour to raise the spiritual level of the people turned to violence because the real aim did not receive the necessary reinforcement at the point of shock and degenerated into dogma.

Our understanding of situations can be greatly increased by relating them to this octave structure, making use of the Tonic Sol-fa notation. In any development we can assign to each stage the appropriate note in its particular octave and in so doing can appreciate its potentialities. We can see whether it is near the beginning or the end of the pattern, or whether it is at the point of shock where some reinforcement will be required.

The notes of an octave can be played in either direction. The sequence shown in Fig. 4 is an ascending octave involving progress from coarser to finer quality. The reverse sequence would constitute a descending octave which is exercised in any creative process in which the development involves progressively more detail, and the Universe is a structure containing an enormous interplay of octaves of both types, of widely varying magnitude.

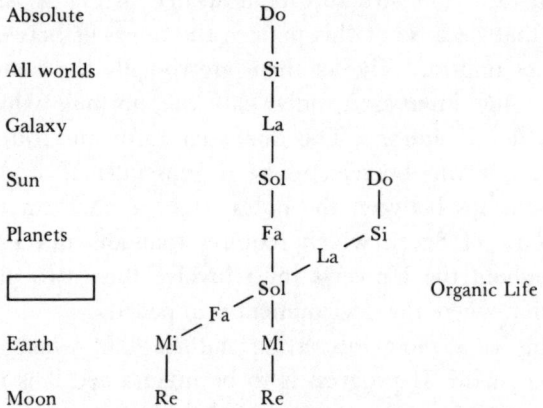

Absolute		Do	
All worlds		Si	
Galaxy		La	
Sun		Sol	Do
Planets		Fa	Si
			La
☐		Sol	Organic Life
	Fa		
Earth	Mi	Mi	
Moon	Re	Re	

Figure 5

The great octave is the Ray of Creation itself, the hierarchy of world-orders discussed earlier (Chapter 3). Since this is a creative process the successive levels will constitute the notes of a descending octave, as shown in Fig. 5. There will be two places of constriction. That between Do and Si is overcome by the will of the Absolute, but that between Fa and Mi requires some additional impetus. It was said, you will remember, that the influences from the higher levels could not reach the earth without the introduction of some medium through which they could be transmitted, and that this was the function of organic life.

We can now see how this is necessary to provide the necessary reinforcement at the place of shock and enable the development to proceed.

Actually, the additional impetus is supplied by means of a 'side octave' originating from the Solar level, World 12. This comprises a succession of subsidiary intelligences which at the notes La, Sol, Fa create the manifestations of organic life on earth and then blend into the notes Mi and Re of the main octave. We need not be concerned with the detail, save to note that this side octave provides a ladder up which energy can pass from the lower regions back to the level of the Sun and so replenish the system.

The Ray of Creation is the prime example of a descending octave but there are innumerable similar patterns at every level of the Universe. The affairs of everyday life depend almost entirely on the development of aims of one kind or another which involve descending octaves, many of which are never properly completed. As a simple example, consider the steps involved in making a table, as illustrated below.

The process will start with the intention, which will then be developed in the imagination in increasing detail, culminating in a specific design. But there is yet no physical manifestation. The octave has reached the point of shock and to proceed further actual materials will have to be acquired together with the necessary tools. If this is done the design can be translated into hardware and if the necessary skill is available there may be produced an actual table. This would be the interpretation of the original idea at a lower and thereby less intelligent level (because a table cannot itself design further tables).

This is a hypothetical example to illustrate the character of a descending octave. If the octave is not reinforced at the points of shock nothing happens, and life is full of incomplete octaves which remain in the imagination. In this example the nature of the shock is easy to see, but in the many psychological octaves of life this is not so, and we experience only a sense of disappoint-

	Do	Idea of table	
Decision to	==		
proceed	Si	All possible forms of table	Creative
	La	Particular type of table	thought
	Sol	Specific requirements	and sketches
	Fa	Detailed design	
Materials	==		
	Mi	Preparation of materials	
	Re	Fabrication	Physical form
	Do	Actual table	

ment and frustration. The concept of the octave pattern gives one a clue as to the reason for the failure and indicates possible solutions.

Often the necessary shock can be provided by using another Centre, i.e. doing something quite different. If one is finding difficulty with an intellectual problem for instance, one can break off into some physical activity or perhaps try some painting or music. We have to find the appropriate shock for ourselves, which we begin to learn when we recognise the existence of the many interwoven octaves in life.

Descending octaves involve stages of progressively lower quality, a transition from finer to coarser material. This is the process of creation and it necessarily starts from an active intention, i.e. an active Do. An ascending octave, on the other hand, can only start from a passive Do, an aim which is subservient to a higher level of understanding. If the octave proceeds there will be a gradual transformation from coarse to finer substances (not necessarily physical).

Life contains many ascending octaves, mostly unrecognised. A particular instance is the process of digestion in which coarse physical food becomes transformed into the intangible 'psychic' materials of thought and feeling, which we will discuss in detail later. In addition there are psychological octaves which can raise our level of being if they start from a passive Do – the acknowledgment of higher authority – and if the necessary shocks are administered at the right points. This is, in fact, more important with ascending octaves because while in a descending octave the absence of the required shock will simply cause the octave to peter out, in an ascending octave progress will continue in a wrong direction as in the case of the Spanish Inquisition cited earlier.

The most significant aspect of an ascending octave, however, is that it is, and can only be, the ascent of an already-created ladder. The progress will be by a succession of triads; but if any note is to be raised in quality this can only happen by the influence of a still higher level, which must already exist. This again will be discussed later, but we can begin to understand the interplay of octaves in the living Universe. At every level energy is transmitted downwards through descending octaves and is then returned through ascending octaves of transformation.

II

Hydrogens

We live in a Universe of qualities, of which we are very indifferently aware. Our ordinary values are almost entirely based on quantities. We are accustomed to measurements of number – of weight, of distance, of time and the like; and we do not see that this is illusion. Plato, in the Timaeus Myth which deals with the creation, discusses the pattern (involving the Law of Three) and then says, 'But since this pattern, which is eternal, could not be joined to any created thing God made an image of eternity progressing according to number – to wit Time'.

The emotional mind is aware of a different scale of values involving the intangible factor of quality. The dictionary defines quality as 'degree of excellence' – but relative to what? What distinguishes a piece of period furniture from a mass-produced article which may be functionally superior? The quality of the period piece would be derived from the work which went into it, the care and skill of the craftsman who made it, and the affection and delight with which it is impregnated. So with great music or works of art which are permeated by the emotions of their creators. Yet we value them today in terms of what they will fetch in the market. We rate a diamond highly for its adornment, yet place no value on the air we breathe, without which we could not survive. Our values are upside down.

How then can we assess quality? It clearly cannot be measured in material terms, but we can perhaps relate it to Swedenborg's doctrine of uses. In such context everything will have a specific and possibly identifiable value determined by its place and purpose in the Universe. This is an aspect of an already created structure containing a vast assembly of energy-matters of which only a very small proportion is physical in character.

Science tells us that matter and energy are both manifestations of vibrations of some kind; but we must not suppose that the physical vibrations perceived by the senses are the only kind that exist. We can, in fact, envisage that the created Universe embodies a vast spectrum of vibrations ranging from the very finest and most rapid, through a succession of slower and denser forms. However, as one would expect, the spectrum is not continuous but develops in discrete steps in accordance with the Law of Seven, producing three consecutive octaves of radiation from the Absolute to the Moon in the Ray of Creation.

This is an idea of considerable practical value and was developed by Gurdjieff in what he called the Table of Hydrogens. In doing so he borrowed the language of the mediaeval alchemists to indicate the quality of the force involved in any operation. In these terms a substance which conducts active force is called a carbon, while one conducting passive force is called an oxygen. The conductor of the third or neutralising force is then called a nitrogen. These terms were adopted by the alchemists because the actual chemical elements bearing these names possess properties having a certain analogy with the forces in a triad. Carbon is the active element in a large number of chemical compounds. Oxygen is a co-operative element very ready to combine with others, while nitrogen can combine with either.

Let us now see how a chain of triads can develop from the octaves of radiation. Three forces will be necessary, to which for the first triad we can assign the values 1, 2 and 3. These must then be conducted by the notes Do, Si, La of the first octave. The Do will conduct active force and so act as a carbon. The passive force however, must be conducted by the note La because the third force must occupy an intermediate position, so that it will be conducted by the note Si, as shown in Fig. 6. Thus the three forces do not operate in sequence, but in the order 1, 3, 2 – an arrangement which is called the cosmic dance.

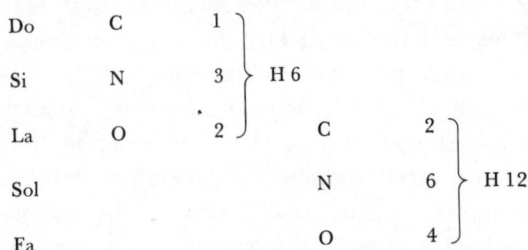

Do	C	1	⎫			
Si	N	3	⎬ H 6			
La	O	2	⎭	C	2	⎫
Sol				N	6	⎬ H 12
Fa				O	4	⎭

Figure 6

These three forces, being in the right relationship, will then produce a resultant which we can designate by the number 6, being the sum of the numbers of the forces. This is a neutral entity, having a specific existence which Gurdjieff called a hydrogen – a purely alchemical term having no connection with the hydrogen of chemistry.

This triad can then generate a further triad, using the notes La, Sol, Fa. The note La will change its role and conduct active force, so acting as a carbon in the second triad; but the intensity of the force will not be changed. It will still have the value 2, so that the forces in this offspring must be designated 2, 4 and 6 respectively resulting in a second hydrogen having the number 12. The process continues with a succession of triads which will produce resultants of increasing coarseness, indicated by the doubling of the hydrogen number at each stage.

However, the first two stages in the development are utterly beyond human comprehension so that for practical purposes we must commence with the highest energy-matter available to (and actually existing in) man. This is the third triad, which will be seen from Fig. 7 to correspond with the level of the Galaxy from which man originates. Hence we take this as the first practical triad and start our numbering from here; so that this becomes, in our scale, hydrogen 6, which has the quality of conscious energy (for us).

Absolute	Do		
	Si		
	La		
All worlds	Sol		
	Fa		
Galaxy	—	H6	Absolute for man
	Mi		
	Re	H12	
Sun	Do		
	Si	H24	Psychic energies
	La		
	Sol	H48	
Planets	Fa		
	—	H96	Vital energy
	Mi		
	Re	H192	Air
Earth	Do		
	Si	H384	Water
	La		
	Sol	H768	Food for man
	Fa		
	—	H1536	Wood
	Mi		
	Re	H3072	Stone
Moon	Do		

Figure 7

This is then followed by a succession of increasingly coarse energy-matters as shown in Fig. 7. The first three are what are called psychic energies. These are the energies which sustain the operation of the various Centres which control the physical and psychological activities of the body. Next is a curious hydrogen sometimes called 'animal magnetism', which is the vital energy necessary to maintain the life of the body; and the table then concludes with five hydrogens of a material quality appertaining to the physical world. The designations are necessarily very broad. H 192, for example, called 'air', is the quality of any

73

gaseous material and the names in general must be taken as indications.

The important aspect of the table of hydrogens is that the successive stages are not compatible in quality. The constitution of the vital energy force, H 96, is clearly of an entirely different order from any of the physical hydrogens. There is, in fact, a change of state at each level, so that the various hydrogens are not just degrees of excellence of the same thing but are separate and distinct energy-matters having their appropriate place in the created Universe.

The assignment of numerical values to these separate entities provides a convenient representation of their scale, and identifies their place and use in the structure. They are the energies which sustain the directing intelligence of the level of their existence. We do not, perhaps, think of physical materials as having a mind, but actually they are assemblies of molecules and atoms which gradually become exhausted and have to be renewed. This replenishment is directed by an appropriate intelligence which is sustained by the force of the corresponding hydrogen.

We can possibly understand this better in connection with the three 'psychic' hydrogens, H 12, H 24 and H 48. These psychological hydrogens, which are beyond the perceptions of the senses, are the energies which sustain the several intelligences or minds which direct our behaviour. H 48 is the energy of the formatory mind, the mind which directs our conventional and stereotyped thinking. H 24 is the energy which is used by the Instinctive and Moving Centres and should be used by Emotional Centre though in practice this Centre all too often works with an inferior quality of energy, like running a highly-tuned racing car on two-star petrol.

H 12 is a still higher quality of energy with which the Sex Centre, with all its tremendous potentialities, should work. However, it rarely does. Its precious energy is stolen by the other Centres which, as said earlier, then work with an undue and dangerous fervour. It can also be used by the inner parts of the Emotional Centre in which case it can communicate with a cosmic intelligence called the Higher Emotional Centre which works with the same hydrogen.

The highest energy available to man is H 6. This is entirely cosmic in character, concerned with an intelligence of Divine quality called the Higher Intellectual Centre. Its function in man is to transmit conscious influences through the structure so that it constitutes the spiritual driving force. Contact with this intelligence, however, is possible only through the development and purification of the inner parts of our individual Centres.

Now, while we can appreciate that these psychic energies will be of different quality there is a very practical aspect of their discontinuity in their different rates of operation. This can be seen by observing the behaviour of the Centres, which work with markedly different speeds. The slowest is the formatory part of Intellectual Centre which is concerned with rational thinking. This works with H 48, which is a very slow energy. Though we may not realise it the formation of coherent thought takes an appreciable time. Consider, for instance, the simple act of walking. If this is to be worked out in detail we will have to decide exactly where to place the feet and which muscles must be used – an operation which will occupy many seconds of time. But Moving Centre, which works with H 24, performs the actions in a fraction of a second (once it has been suitably educated).

There is an even greater disparity in the operations of Instinctive Centre, which also works with H 24. A glass of brandy will produce an almost instantaneous sensation of warmth. Yet to do so it has had to undergo a series of elaborate chemical transformations which would take hours in a laboratory. Similarly the Emotional Centre creates instant feelings of like or dislike, of joy, of anxiety and fear, etc., without any thought.

It is said that H 24 is 30,000 times quicker than H 48. This is a magical number which will be discussed later when we come to consider the Cosmoses (Chapter 13), but it is clear that the ordinary processes of thought are very cumbersome by comparison with the other faculties. However, the Intellectual Centre can work with H 24 if it operates in harmony with Emotional Centre. This creates the instant and wordless cognition which we call intuition. Moreover, the inner parts of Centres can work with still finer hydrogens, producing even faster reactions, as with a juggler who has effectively more time at his disposal. However, one must not expect a sudden and complete change of level. As one becomes more conscious the Centres begin to operate with a mixture of hydrogens, providing an intermediate quality of energy which may gradually become purer.

The impressions received by the senses take a small time to travel through the nerves to the brain, but the subsequent interpretation of the information depends upon the level of the directing intelligence. This has laid down patterns of associations which are then interrogated by the brain in accordance with its established programme. The logical mind creates elaborately detailed associations which have then to be examined in turn. This is H 48 thinking, which is slow and ponderous, though necessary in exploring any new subject. However, if the lighter energy of H 24 is used it will provide modified programmes which will discard much of the detail and see short-cuts in the interrogation, so that the interpretations are immeasurably quicker.

The associations in the Instinctive and Moving Centres are much simpler and are scanned by the appropriate mind much more rapidly; and this applies even more to Emotional Centre which in its pure state is concerned only with patterns of relationships in the Universe which the emotional mind, using the timeless energies of H 24 and H 12, can recognise as a whole.

Evidently, these higher hydrogens are of great potentiality but although they exist we must not assume that they are automatically available. We have to establish contact with them by our

own efforts, involving the conscious use of the processes of transformation in the body.

It is clear that this table of hydrogens is no arbitrary classifica-
tion, but is an expression of the very nature of the Universe. It
illustrates, for example, how the vivifying forces are transmitted
through the created structure in a series of descending triads,
producing a succession of distinct manifestations of progressively
lower potentiality, but specifically applicable to the conditions
at their level. One can see, for instance, in physical terms that
air, which is of the quality of H 192, has a degree of freedom
not possessed by water, H 384; but water is a necessary medium
for fishes which cannot live in air.

We are not aware of this devolving process as such. We only
perceive the results in the apparently separate manifestations of
the familiar world. Yet we can recognise that matter left to
itself degenerates into disorder so that in a living Universe there
must be some mechanism of replenishment; and this is actually
achieved by processes of transformation at each level. But no
material or energy can be raised in quality except by the
influence of some higher level, which must already exist. The
table of hydrogens shows that such levels do, in fact, exist so that
the necessary transformations can be produced by a succession
of ascending triads. This indeed is a little recognised but essential
activity in the Universe, which will be discussed next.

12

Transformation

One of the activities of the natural world to which we give little thought is the continual process of transformation by which new energies are created to offset the processes of decay. There are many examples of this in Nature. There are the transformations of seeds into plants, of eggs into birds, or frogs or even men. The growth of green vegetation involves the transformation of light into matter by the process of photosynthesis, and there are many similar activities of which in the ordinary way we are quite unaware.

There are various examples of metamorphosis, such as the transformation of a caterpillar into a butterfly. The caterpillar lives on the surface of leaves, in what is effectively a two-dimensional world, in which it feeds and grows until at a certain stage it wraps itself in a cocoon and goes into a state of suspended animation from which it emerges as a butterfly, a being of an entirely different order. It has an additional degree of freedom within a three-dimensional world. It feeds on different substances and is itself food for different creatures. It has the possibility of laying eggs, which a caterpillar does not have, and it is interesting to note that these eggs hatch out as caterpillars so that this transformation, this change of level, is something organised by Nature for a purpose.

Even more remarkable is the development of a fertilised cell into a child, a process involving a whole octave of transformations, culminating at the appropriate time in the emergence of a being of a different order – a transformation from the cosmos of cells to the cosmos of man. The very essence of transformation, in fact, is change of state from one level to a higher one.

Now though we are normally only vaguely aware of the fact, the human body is an extraordinary transforming machine. It maintains itself by the intake of food of various kinds which it transforms into the energies required for its daily operations. This is directed by the intelligence of Instinctive Centre, which we accept as of right, being only concerned if something goes wrong – usually from our own stupidity.

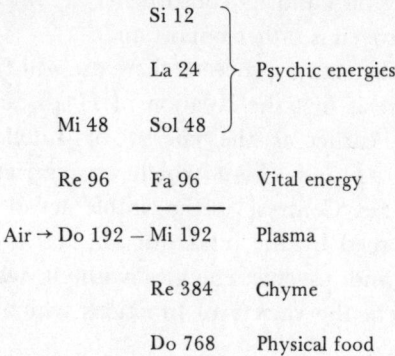

	Si 12	
	La 24	Psychic energies
Mi 48	Sol 48	
Re 96	Fa 96	Vital energy
Air → Do 192 – Mi 192		Plasma
	Re 384	Chyme
	Do 768	Physical food

Figure 8

This food is then taken into the stomach, as H 768. Here, by the action of enzymes already present in the system it is transformed into a liquid material called chyme, of the quality of H 384; and this in turn is converted to gaseous material H 192, as shown in Fig. 8. These two stages constitute the first two notes of an ascending octave; but here there is the place of constriction at which the progress is impeded. Hence it is necessary to reinforce the energy of the note Mi by the introduction of some external material of the same quality, and this is provided by the intake of air by the lungs. We know from experience that we have to breathe to live, but we do not normally realise the way in which this is necessary to reinforce the digestive processes. Moreover, this second food has to be of the right quality. Fresh air invigorates the body. Stale or foul air quickly causes indigestion or even illness.

Given this renewed impetus the octave then proceeds to the creation of Fa 96. Here there is a complete change of quality. Up to this point the transformations have been physical, and could be reproduced in a laboratory. But this transition from Mi to Fa has produced an energy of a different order, namely the vital energy which sustains the life of the body. Science does not know what this is. It only knows that if there is not enough vitality the body dies and its constituents decompose. Evidently this strange hydrogen is rather important.

However, as the octave proceeds there are still further changes of quality. There is first the creation of H 48, at the note Sol, which we saw earlier is the energy of Intellectual Centre, followed by H 24 and H 12 which are concerned with the Emotional and Sex Centres. So the simple act of eating a piece of bread, reinforced by the intake of air, has created a whole range of vital and psychic energies without which the body could not perform the variety of functions which we take completely for granted.

Yet all this is a mechanical operation, a cosmic process which was programmed by the intelligence of organic life when the body was brought into being. It is automatic and requires no attention beyond the procuring of the necessary food and air. But esoteric teaching says that there is a further kind of transformation possible for man which is not automatic but requires conscious attention. This requires the conscious intake of a third food which we normally do not recognise as such, namely the food of impressions; and we are told that if this food can be eaten it will produce a further and more powerful supply of the higher hydrogens.

What do we mean by impressions? Superficially, they are items of information provided by the senses. If there were no senses we would certainly not receive any impressions, but I think it is rather deeper than this. For one thing, the same event, the same situation, can evoke quite different impressions according to the state of the recipient. So it seems to me that in impressions there must be some element of meaning. Ouspensky defines an impression as the smallest unit of thought, sensation or emotion, which one might paraphrase by calling it the smallest unit of awareness. In this light we can see that impressions can be received from many parts of the Universe, having qualities ranging over the whole spectrum of hydrogens.

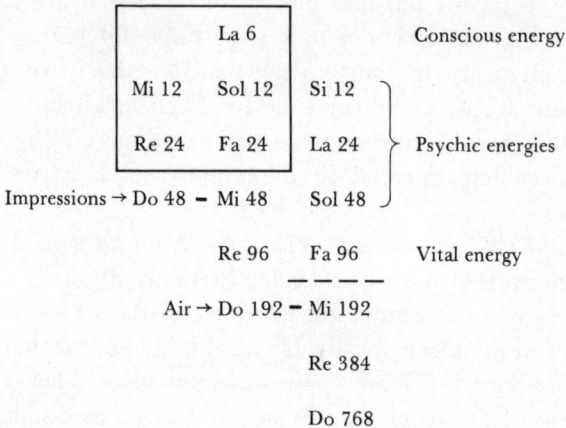

		La 6		Conscious energy
Mi 12	Sol 12	Si 12 ⎫
Re 24	Fa 24	La 24 ⎬	Psychic energies
Impressions → Do 48 — Mi 48	Sol 48 ⎭
	Re 96	Fa 96	Vital energy
	— — — —
Air → Do 192 — Mi 192
	Re 384
	Do 768

Figure 9

Nevertheless, we can say that, as an average, impressions are of the quality of H 48, because they are normally recognised by the Intellectual Centre which works with this hydrogen. Many of the impressions which assail us every moment make little or no impact because our attention is otherwise engaged. But if a few are actually taken in they can start a third octave at the level of H 48 and proceed to the notes Re 24 and Mi 12, as shown in Fig. 9. These will be two psychic hydrogens additional to those produced by the mechanical octave of Fig. 8. Moreover, because they are at the beginning of their octave they will have much greater potentiality.

Yet this is only part of the story. The air which we breathe to provide the reinforcement at the Mi-Fa gap in the food octave will start its own octave and sound the notes Re 96 and Mi 48, so enriching the energies produced by the mechanical octave; but here the progress will stop because again there will be a missing semitone. However, if the impressions octave has commenced it will provide the necessary shock in the air octave which will then proceed, producing a further supply of psychic hydrogens, and even a small amount of conscious energy La 6, as illustrated in Fig. 9.

Clearly, the body has unsuspected intricacies. It is sometimes likened to a 3-storey factory producing three different grades of energy – physical, vital and psychic; and for this it will require appropriate foods, of which two are freely available but the third – the food of impressions – has to be specially prepared, and is absolutely essential to the proper development of the organism.

It is said that we cannot exist without impressions, but this can be interpreted too superficially. Certainly the body needs a constant supply of information provided by the senses, which is then interpreted mechanically by the brain. But we have seen that impressions are more than sense reactions. They contain an element of awareness, and if we are to live, as distinct from merely existing, we must learn how to use these impressions as food.

There are two requirements here. The first is the need for discrimination because not all impressions are of suitable quality. We are bombarded by impressions from many parts of the Universe but we do not have to accept them indiscriminately. We can develop a taste which will select those which are good food and reject those which are harmful or poisonous, just as Instinctive Centre will spit out bad physical food. We are curiously insensitive in our choice of impressions. Some people rush to the scene of an accident to wallow in unpleasant sensations; and there is the constant intake of filth from the internal impressions generated by internal considering. Really, we should be more intelligent!

Impressions which are acceptable then have to be digested. Just as physical food provides no nourishment until it is transformed by the action of ferments in the stomach, so impressions have to be subjected to the influence of psychological ferments, for which purpose we have to organise a kind of psychological stomach; and this is the second requirement, of which we are usually unaware.

Now, this is clearly a conscious exercise, requiring a different quality of attention from that which suffices for life affairs. It is called First Conscious Shock, as distinct from the shock of breathing in the food octave which is automatic. We have to submit to the direction of the deeper levels of the mind which can interpret impressions in a different way, not in terms of life requirements but in relationship to the real world.

When we speak of deeper levels of the mind we are apt to forget that these are intelligencies of a different order, operating in the Astral world and aware of the situations of life all together, not separated by passing time. This is what Christ called *metanoia* which does not mean repentance but the use of a mind beyond the ordinary.

If the incoming impressions are subservient to this higher level of intelligence they can form the first note of an ascending octave commencing with Do 48. The next note will be Re 24, which is of a higher quality; but for this to happen there has to be present a still higher hydrogen, H 12, and if this conducts active force we have a triad as shown in Fig. 10. The 'carbon' of this triad will be esoteric teaching of some sort, which by conducting conscious influences will create a substance of intermediate quality, H 24, which is emotional understanding. This in turn can become the passive element in a further triad subservient to a still higher intelligence of the quality of H 6, which for us is Divine; and this can produce H 12, at the note Mi of the octave, which then stops unless a further reinforcement, called Second Conscious Shock, can be provided; but we are told that this must not be attempted, or even considered until one has mastered the technique of the First Conscious Shock.

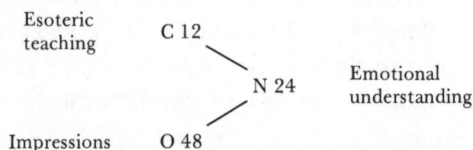

Esoteric
teaching   C 12

                            N 24   Emotional
                                        understanding

Impressions   O 48

Figure 10

This whole concept of the food octaves must be interpreted emotionally, i.e. as a pattern of relationships – and as such it is intensely stimulating. The significant aspect of the pattern is that no transformation is possible without the influence of something higher in quality, so that the various stages in the several octaves are, in fact, ascents of an already-existing ladder. All the hydrogens discussed are already available, but their energy is continually being dissipated so that they have to be replenished; and this is the purpose of the food octaves, some of which are of cosmic dispensation, but the more important ones involve individual effort.

How can we avail ourselves of these opportunities in practice? We must have a positive conviction that conscious interpretation of impressions is entirely possible, and to the extent that it is achieved the events of life acquire a new character. Everything appears lighter and more vivid, embracing much wider horizons; but it is clear that this state cannot be attained by 'taking thought' because this is an exercise of the Personality, whereas transformation is only possible through the influence of a higher level of intelligence.

In our normal condition, however, the demands of Personality are so clamorous that we cannot hear the higher influences even though we can accept intellectually that they exist. We have to sacrifice many of our cherished attitudes – including the firmly established belief in our rights – to make room for more conscious interpretations of events. If someone says or does something which annoys me I shall resent it, possibly violently, but certainly internally, and add it to the list of accounts which I make against him or her. Yet if I can begin to mistrust the feeling of my own importance I may see the possibility that I asked for it, that it was some action or attitude on my part which called forth the unpleasant remark. I may perhaps begin to observe more objectively my reactions to the events of the day, and see that they contain the possibility of different interpretations.

For a long time it is impossible to catch the event as it happens, so one can only make this possible transformation in retrospect. Sometimes one may recognise that the Personality has behaved in its usual arrogant manner, and see that if it is allowed to go on acting in that way there is going to be a chain reaction, and possibly a really unpleasant explosion. Usually, however, the event and its consequences are over before we have even started to be aware of it. So one has to begin to start transforming impressions in retrospect. Certainly at night, before one goes to sleep, one can review the events of the day and observe how the Personality reacted and visualise the different situation if the behaviour had been directed by a higher level of the mind, using conscious interpretations instead of life associations.

If this is done as a conscious exercise, rather than a mere recollection, it is possible to re-interpret the situation which will actually transform the event. This is possible because the events of the day are still there. We think of the experiences of the morning as having passed. We think of lunch time, or 5 o'clock, as having passed. Yet the whole of the day is still present in the Astral world. All the experiences of the day still exist in our time-body in the domain of Eternity. So that it is literally possible to transform impressions after the event. Indeed, for a long time it is the only thing we can do.

Moreover, this possibility can be exercised way back in the past. If one can awaken memory in one's time-body dispassionately, without judgment or guilt, it is possible to transform the meaning of experiences of long ago, and this can gradually change the quality of the whole life. One begins to develop an expanded awareness of the present moment, so that the still powerful interpretations of habit are accompanied by a conscious understanding which begins to take charge.

It may be asked why this is necessary. Why should we not be content with our customary reactions? Simply because this would be a betrayal of one's purpose, an unprofitable experiment serving only the cosmic requirements of organic life. As Christ said, a tree which does not bear good fruit is cut down and cast into the fire. But what fruit is required of us? It is the creation of the higher hydrogens of which we have been speaking. With our customary self-centred thinking we regard these as belonging to us, but the truth is that these are cosmic energies, of which a small portion is lent to us during our life. We are required to provide some replenishment of these energies by trying to live our lives consciously.

There is a further aspect of transformation which seems to be little understood, namely that any such operation leaves a residue. If a piece of paper is burnt its material is converted into a higher (gaseous) state but it leaves behind an ash, which is of lower quality. The food we eat is refined by the digestive processes, but the residue is evacuated and serves a lower level, being food for bacteria. There are similar unsuspected residues in the higher orders of transformation. As Meister Eckhart, the 14th century mystic, says in one of his sermons, 'All the work and waste of Heaven is caught midway in the sink of Earth'.

In his strange book *All and Everything* Gurdjieff says that everything is food for something else, and that man's function is to provide food for the moon – meaning that level of intelligence called World 96 which is the growing tip of the Ray of Creation. He says further that if this is done by conscious transformations it is only the waste products which are so used; and in the process a man creates for himself the materials necessary for the organisation of the higher bodies in himself.

This idea is often misinterpreted. It is said that at death the energies accumulated by the negative emotions and other activities of the False Personality go to the moon; but this is a very coarse food of which the moon has more than enough and its development is held up by the shortage of its real nourishment.

This then is the task – to provide conscious interpretations of the events of life, which by the very act immeasurably broadens our horizons. We spoke earlier of the transition of a caterpillar from its surface world to the three-dimensional world of the butterfly. By inference we can see that our own three-dimensional existence could be merely a preparation for the inhabitation of a world of higher dimensions, a world which includes time as part of the structure, just as the dimensions of space are part of the structure which our senses recognise. We are equipped to live in a world of a higher order of intelligence; but the attainment of this state involves a transition which is not automatic. Individual effort is required.

13

The Cosmoses

We have spoken on various occasions of the different levels in the Universe, which we are told are discontinuous. This means that the levels do not simply merge into one another but involve a change of state. The prime example of levels is the world-orders in the Ray of Creation, each of which, we are told, has its own unique quality of intelligence and manifestation. They all obey the same fundamental laws but on different scales, and one of the significant differences between the successive levels is that each has its own scale of time. We have seen, for example, that in the Astral world time as we know it does not exist.

This important aspect of the world-orders is illustrated by the concept of cosmoses. The word cosmos means order, and we often refer to the Universe as the cosmos. Gurdjieff, however, said that according to ancient, but largely forgotten, legend there is associated with the world-orders a succession of individual cosmoses, which are structures embodying the practical implications of the laws of the particular level. Each of them is a living structure subject to specific rules and constraints which are basically the same but operate on appropriately different scales. We can understand, for instance, that the cosmos of man, i.e. humanity as a whole, has to conform to certain requirements such as the need to breathe, to eat, to sleep periodically, and so forth. We shall see that similar rules apply at their level in all the cosmoses.

Gurdjieff originally postulated seven cosmoses ranging from the Protocosmos, the cosmos of the Absolute, down to the Microcosmos, the cosmos of man. The first five correspond with the unmanifest world-orders as far as the Astral level, but here there is a divergence because the next two are physical, corresponding with organic life and man respectively, as shown in Table 1. Ouspensky later extended the series to include increasingly small material constituents down to the ultimately small sub-atomic particles. However, in seeking to establish these sub-microcosmoses one can become involved in unnecessary detail and in Table 1 I have only included three, namely cells, atoms and electrons, which have structures conforming to the pattern of discontinuous levels. No random assembly of electrons will create an atom, nor will a mere profusion of atoms constitute a cell. In each case a directing intelligence of a higher order is involved. Moreover, the physical dimensions and vibration rates of these three cosmoses are related by the curious factor of 30,000 which we will discuss shortly, so that they form with the Deutero, Meso and Trito cosmoses a period of seven relative to the scale of man, just as Gurdjieff's original seven cosmoses constitute a period centred around the Sun.

Table 1   *The Ten Cosmoses*

	Representation	*Governing World-order*
Protocosmos	Absolute uncreate	1
Ayocosmos	All worlds	3
Macrocosmos	The galaxy	6 (Divine)
Deuterocosmos	Sun	12 (Spiritual)
Mesocosmos	Planets, including earth	24 (Astral)
Tritocosmos	Organic life	Linking intelligence
1st Microcosmos	Physical Man	
2nd ,,	Cells	48 (Phenomenal)
3rd ,,	Atoms	
4th ,,	Electrons	

Now, while this may seem an arbitrary series, it contains an unsuspected pattern. But to understand this we must start with something within our normal comprehension, namely man himself. He is a living being who thinks, breathes, eats, sleeps and eventually dies, and he can be distinguished as an organism by the time involved in these various activities. We can, in fact, choose four characteristic times, namely the time of sensory perception, the time of breath, the period of waking and sleeping and the time of life.

The last three are fairly easily defined. We normally breathe in and out about twenty times a minute so that the time of breath can be taken, on average, as 3 seconds. Our time of waking and sleeping is 24 hours, involving a period of activity followed by a period of recuperation, while the time of life is of the order of 80 years. The time of perception is less familiar. We usually assume that our perceptions are instantaneous but actually the physical changes which the senses detect have to be sustained for a certain small but definite length of time before there is any response. Anything of shorter duration does not register, and it seems that this critical time is of the order of 1/10,000 second.

Hence the four relevant times for man are shown in the table below.

Table 2 *Characteristic Times*

Quickest perception	1/10,000 second
Breath	3 seconds
Day and night	24 hours
Time of life	80 years

Now, these times have a significant relationship to each other, namely that they differ by a factor of approximately 30,000. The ratio is not exact, but neither are the times. Actually the number 30,000 is a magical figure derived from esoteric knowledge. Mathematically it is the ratio between a moment of time in any given world order and the equivalent moment in a world of a higher dimension. The significance of this relationship becomes apparent if we try to estimate the characteristic times in the adjacent cosmoses.

Gurdjieff said in his laconic way, 'Time is Breath'. What will be the time of breath for organic life? This corresponds with the time of waking and sleeping in man, which is 24 hours. All Nature, whether plant, bird or beast, undergoes rhythmic changes of condition once a day. Plants absorb carbon dioxide from the air and convert it, in the presence of light, into substance, but at night they return it to the air and rhythmic actions such as this operate throughout organic life.

This means that the time-scale of organic life is 30,000 times longer than ours, which provides a new set of characteristic times as shown in Table 3. On this scale the time of quickest perception is 3 seconds, which is an unfamiliar idea. Yet plants do not possess a nervous system. Their internal communication is by chemical changes and experiments show that their reaction times are of this order. We do not know what the 'day' of 80 years implies, while the life of $2\frac{1}{2}$ million years seems much too short. Yet in the present context the lifetime of this (or any) entity is simply the time during which its energy gradually becomes exhausted, when it dies and is replaced by fresh creation; and clearly this may take place hundreds of times in the slow evolution of life on earth.

Nor is the cosmos of organic life concerned only with the physical manifestations of Nature. It is the implementation of an intelligence of a high order concerned with psychological and spiritual activities of which we are mostly unaware. We must not interpret it with the literal mind.

Conversely, the time-scale of the cellular world appears to be 30,000 times quicker than ours. The ordinary cells of the body are not everlasting but are continually dying and being replaced by new ones – except for the brain cells which are a special breed lasting the whole life of the body. The common cells, however, only have a life of about 24 hours, so that they have to be replaced roughly once a day – of course, not all at once.

However, during their life they will need appropriate periods of recuperation. Have you ever wondered why we blink our eyelids every few seconds? It is to allow the cells of the eyes to sleep and if the eyelids are held open (as in certain forms of torture) it causes agony. The day of a cell, in fact, can be taken as of the order of 3 seconds. The time of breath we do not know, but cells are nourished by an interchange of gases which may well be rhythmic in character taking place 10,000 times every second. So again we can see a similar pattern of characteristic times, as in Table 3.

Table 3   *The Adjacent Cosmoses*

Cosmos	Quickest Perception	Breath	Day and Night	Life
Organic Life	3 sec	24 hours	80 years	2½ million years
Man	1/10,000 sec	3 sec	24 hours	80 years
Cells	1/300 microsec	1/10,000 sec	3 sec	24 hours

The logical mind may quibble with some of the presentation but the concept of the different cosmoses introduces additional meaning into many ordinary situations. It explains, for example, how the much more rapid time-scale of the cellular world permits the elaborate processes of the body to be carried out so quickly that we are hardly aware of them. The blood cells exchange gases in the lungs in a few seconds. If you cut your finger they organise in minutes a repair job which would take us days. All of which goes on without any awareness on our part.

Alternatively, we can see how the time-scale of the Astral world is literally eternal for us. This is the world of the meso-cosmos which you will see from Table 1 is two stages above that of man. Hence its time-scale will be 30,000 x 30,000 = 900 million times longer than ours. In the words of the familiar hymn, 'A thousand ages in Thy sight are but an evening gone'.

It is possible to extend the tables of times in both directions and devise a scale of lifetimes ranging from a few millionths of a second for the electronic cosmos to a fantastic number of years involving 30 figures for the Protocosmos – numbers which do not contribute anything to our understanding. What we can, and indeed must, do is to try to be aware of the cosmoses in which we are most closely concerned. We must feel the wonder of organic life and ourselves within it. How do you regard the environment? As something of no account, a mere background to the constant activity of expectation – or as something which will talk to you if you let it?

Do you feel the cells of your body as living beings? They only live for a day, yet during that time they serve us remarkably faithfully without hope of reward. To them we are as gods. I remember Mrs Nicoll telling me once that having spent a whole day wallowing in negative emotions she realised that by so doing she had condemned the cells of her body to a lifetime of hell; and in quite practical terms, if we go on doing this how can we expect the body to remain healthy?

The cosmoses must not be considered in isolation. For a proper understanding at least three cosmoses must be considered together. This permits the reconciliation of apparent anomalies. For instance, we are told that a higher level of intelligence is quicker in its operations, which seems incompatible with the idea of a longer time-scale.

However, the perceptions of a higher level are more comprehensive. A slow-witted person will see only one thing at a time. A more quick-witted individual, having a wider range of knowledge, will take in many more impressions in exactly the same time. We have all experienced moments of higher consciousness in conditions of emergency such as a motor accident when the whole situation, in a wealth of detail, passes through our awareness as if in slow motion. There is an expansion of time into a longer time-scale, yet because it all happens in a moment of our time the individual perceptions must be many thousand times quicker.

Hence a moment of perception for the intelligence of organic life involves a whole day of the operations of the cellular cosmos, with ourselves in the middle. We can, in fact, bracket the higher and lower cosmoses together as in Table 4; and similarly if our consciousness were appropriately raised we would be aware in the Astral world and the atomic cosmos simultaneously; and at a still higher level in the cosmoses of the Sun and the electrons of which the sun is composed.

Table 4   *The Seven Cosmoses for Man*

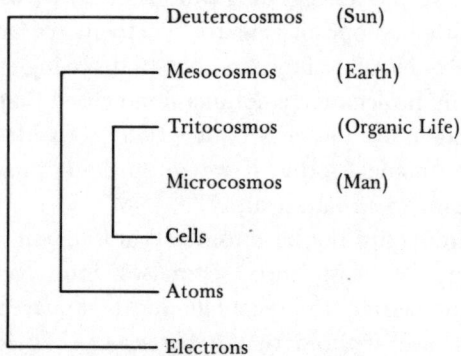

Deuterocosmos	(Sun)
Mesocosmos	(Earth)
Tritocosmos	(Organic Life)
Microcosmos	(Man)
Cells	
Atoms	
Electrons	

Ideas of this kind can awaken the emotional parts of the mind which are concerned with relationships in the Universe; and there are many connections which emerge if one is prepared to stretch the mind. For instance, it will be seen that a day in the cosmos of cells corresponds to the time of breath in man. We can envisage that every individual entity, in the course of its daily existence within its own cosmos, is responsible for some essential manifestation in a higher cosmos of which it may be

94

completely ignorant. This puts a new interpretation on our own daily round which may sometimes seem meaningless but may be fulfilling a necessary requirement at a higher level.

We have to pursue such ideas for ourselves, for as Gurdjieff said when he first spoke of the subject, 'Knowledge begins with the study of the cosmoses'. But it is not an intellectual study. It begins with the realisation of the existence of the cosmoses and the attempt to be present in the three closest at hand – organic life, man and cells. Ultimately the aim is to be aware in the complete series of seven cosmoses from the Sun to Electrons, which would be the consummation of the life.

14

Prayer

Our spiritual endeavours are concerned with raising our level of being; and we know that this can only be achieved by individual effort, which we begin to make in response to the conscious influences which reach us in various ways. However, we soon find that our life associations are of no value in this quest. We need help from higher levels of consciousness, which we are told is available but for which we have to learn how to ask.

This is what is called prayer. The dictionary defines it as 'earnest request', but it is surely relevant to ask to whom the request is addressed. Conventionally, in our state of sleep, we address our prayers to an imagined superior Being who is not only responsible for our creation but is concerned for our welfare and from whom therefore we have a right to ask for help when things become difficult. If our prayers are not immediately answered we are liable to become resentful, or alternatively adopt an attitude of pious resignation to the will of God.

This is unintelligent, and I am often reminded of the comment by the novelist Jack London who was very scornful about the sentimental prayers which small children were encouraged to repeat –

> Now I lay me down to sleep,
> I pray the Lord my soul to keep,

Prayer

> And if I die before I wake,
> I pray the Lord my soul to take.

He would have nothing of this. He said if he had a son he would teach him to say –

> Now I get me up to work,
> I pray to God I shall not shirk,
> And if I die before tonight,
> I pray my work may be all right.

This is surely a much more positive attitude. Prayer is more than a desire to have one's own way. Maurice Nicoll says in *The New Man* that it is the attempt to communicate with a higher level. This is a little more inspiring, but what does it involve? What higher level are we trying to communicate with? I think we forget that such higher level is of an utterly different order. Let us remind ourselves of the Ray of Creation, the hierarchy of world-orders devolving from the Supreme of Absolute Intelligence in a succession of subordinate manifestations. The world-order immediately above the Earth, which we call the Astral world, is not a mere extension of our ordinary conditions, but is a realm which is controlled by laws of a different order. It is not subject, for example, to the laws of passing time and by that very token it has possibilities which are infinite in relation to our ordinary understanding.

It is important to recognise the incommensurability of the successive levels, each of which has different degrees of freedom, different dimensions. The idea of dimensions has acquired a wholly spurious mystique. A dimension is simply a means of measurement in a certain direction. You can understand, for example, that a mite living on the surface of this page would have a certain amount of freedom over the surface but it would have no concept of the possibility of movement out of the surface either upwards or downwards. This would constitute movement in a different (third) dimension, movement in a space which has infinitely greater possibilities. Yet for us this is the normal world which we take as a matter of course.

So this higher level that we are trying to communicate with is a realm having vastly different potentialities and we cannot attempt to communicate with this level of intelligence by using the kind of thinking which we employ for the purposes of life. The associations and attitudes of the Personality are just inadequate. Only the use of the inner mind can conceive the possibility of communicating with this much greater level of intelligence and it is the possession of this inner mind which distinguishes man from the animals. Animals have senses and associations by which they live, but they are not provided with an inner mind, a deeper level of the mind, which can think in categories of a different order.

Of course if one does not believe in the existence of a superior intelligence then no such communication is possible. The door is held firmly closed by the adherence to stereotyped associations and the sort of idle wishing that passes for prayer in conventional terms. This kind of complacent stupidity can only keep the understanding earthbound and prevent any development of the inner mind.

Hence if we wish to understand what prayer is, and what its possibilities are, we must practise *metanoia* – the use of a mind beyond the ordinary. This enables us to see meanings which are obscured by the perfunctory interpretations of habit. You will remember that when Christ was asked by his disciples how they should pray he gave the succinct formula which has become known as the Lord's Prayer, which we repeat without understanding, as if it were some magic rune. (Matthew vi, 9).

It *is* magical, but only if it is spoken as an offering to a higher level. It begins, 'Our Father in Heaven', which is an immediate acknowledgment of a superior Intelligence. Then follow the words, 'Hallowed be Thy name', which is a phrase of the deepest significance. To name anything is to acknowledge it. In life we use names as mere labels, without any awareness of meaning. Here we are told to acknowledge this Intelligence with the greatest awe as something to be made holy in our hearts. What name we use, if we have to assign a name at all, is not important. Different religions have their own names.

The prayer continues, 'Thy kingdom come', usually interpreted as a hope for some future state which will transcend the present evils and cruelties – without any suggestion of payment on our part! The phrase should be taken in conjunction with the following words, 'Thy will be done on earth, as in Heaven', which is not an injunction to accept the fortunes of life with resignation but is an expression of the ancient Hermetic aphorism, 'As above, so below'. Hence there is once again the implication of acknowledgment, recognition of the fact that the affairs of this world are manifestations of the divine plan and a reminder of the obligation incumbent on each one of us to contribute to this plan.

Next is the demand, 'Give us this day our daily bread', which has nothing to do with physical food. The word 'daily' is a mistranslation of the Greek word *epiousios* which means beyond the ordinary – literally 'what is appropriate for the moment'. The phrase is a request to the higher powers to continue to provide us with the events of the day, the impressions which are our richest source of nourishment. Do we see every day as a gift? I doubt it. We see its events mostly as occasions for complaint.

There is then a very significant passage, often rendered very superficially as, 'Forgive us our trespasses'. The wording in the original has a very different meaning. It says, 'Cancel our debts, to the extent that we cancel what (we think) is owed to us'. It never occurs to us that we owe anything for the experiences of life, its joys and happinesses, even the disappointments and hardships which temper our spirit. Yet the very acknowledgment of the obligation is at least a token repayment, and if we continue to do this the whole debt may be cancelled.

The prayer concludes with the strange words, 'Lead us not

99

into temptation but deliver us from evil'. This is usually regarded as two separate requests, but it must be taken as a whole. Temptation is a necessary part of our endeavour. The ancient alchemists likened it to the fire under a crucible which can fuse the random experiences of life into a coherent and valuable alloy. But we ask that we shall not be faced with more than we can bear; and in fact this is granted, for we only encounter situations for which we are ready, if we can see how to use them.

It will be seen that this prayer, which Christ gave as a model, contains no element of personal advantage. It is concerned only with awareness of higher levels with which Essence yearns to communicate. Nearly all life prayers are concerned with the removal of difficulties. Yet these are the life-blood of our existence because it is only by contending with difficulties that our true meaning develops. So the only thing we can legitimately pray for is understanding.

It is sometimes said that the Universe is a structure of response to request; but it must be a possible request, involving obedience to established laws. There are obvious requests which we know cannot be granted at life level, though sometimes physical laws can be transcended by what we call a miracle, which results from direction by a superior level. Normally, however, a life prayer is governed by the laws of the earth level. Spiritual prayer is not.

Actually we are constantly making requests of the Universe. We don't call it prayer; we call it planning. A scientist is continually posing questions to the Universe, which will provide answers depending on the quality of his questions. Prayer, in fact, like every activity, is subject to the Law of Three. The request is first force which will inevitably bring into play a second force of opposition and unless these two are reconciled by an appropriate third force nothing happens. So if the response is not what one expects it means that the request has been wrongly framed. We have to be aware of exactly what has been requested, and we often find that we are getting what we asked for without knowing it. In any case we have to envisage what second force will be involved, i.e. what difficulties will have to be overcome, and perhaps modify the request so that these can be accommodated. This is no more than normal life intelligence.

How much more important this must be with a spiritual request. Most of our prayers are imagination because we are not aware of precisely what we are asking for. I may perhaps pray to be more conscious. What prevents it? My Personality, which wants its own way. This must be made passive so that my feeling of I is offered up to a higher level of intelligence not concerned with the gratification of life demands. Yet there is still a third force required, to make the prayer possible. This will involve payment – payment in effort, in discarding some of the stupidities of desire, the constant internal considering, the continual feeling of being owed.

So if one wants to pray – and we do quite sincerely because we want to raise our level of being – if one wants to formulate any kind of real prayer, ask first of all will it be acceptable to a higher level and secondly have we brought the money with us; because unless we have the prayer cannot be granted. There is no credit in Heaven. They want cash on the nail, which means that we have to begin to accumulate this spiritual money now, before making any attempt to pray.

There are many parables in the Gospels which illustrate this necessity. One of them is the parable of the marriage feast which on the face of it looks very unjust. There was a lord who had prepared a marriage feast and something went wrong and all the appointed guests were unable to be present. So he said to his servants, 'Go out into the highways and byways and bring in whoever you can find, so they may partake of this feast which we have prepared'. Wandering among these guests he comes across a man without a wedding garment and he asks why he has come without proper clothing. The man, unable to reply, is asked to leave. It seems a bit hard doesn't it? But the fact is that we have to have wedding garments prepared *in advance* against the possibility of enlightenment from a higher level.

There is the other parable of the wise and the foolish virgins who are awaiting the arrival of their lord. Five of them took the trouble to see that they had enough oil in their lamps in anticipation. The other five did not bother, so when the lord arrived suddenly they were scurrying in all directions trying to get oil and of course they could not. There are many parables which illustrate this need to prepare now, to begin to acquire spiritual money, not for a specific purpose but in anticipation. If I say I will make certain kinds of effort to increase my stature this is working for result and will be useless. There has to be virtually no personal considering in prayer.

Now even supposing one has begun to see what real prayer means, this is no more than the starting point because the essential requisite of prayer is that it must be persistent. It is no good offering up a prayer and then just waiting for something to happen. One has to go on re-iterating the prayer. This is illustrated in the parable of the importunate widow who had some grievance about which she pestered the judge. For a long time he paid no heed, until in desperation he said, 'Oh, for goodness' sake do what this woman wants'. We have to use the same kind of persistence, which Nicoll calls shameless impudence. It is as if the gods were too occupied with running their part of the Universe to be bothered with our puny requests, even though we think they are very sincere. So we have to persist with the prayer.

One can understand this in another way because what we are asking for is a transformation of understanding; but any transformation can only come about when a certain quantum of energy has been accumulated. If you boil a kettle the water does not immediately turn to steam. There has to be an accumulation of heat energy in the water until the molecules have become sufficiently energised to change their state into steam. If you don't maintain the heat for sufficiently long nothing happens.

The water simply cools down again and you have to start afresh. It is like this with prayer. It is no good just offering up a prayer, however sincere, in expectation of an instant answer. The pressure has to be maintained.

This is not something that can be done once a day mechanically. Tibetans use prayer wheels, cylinders containing the invocation *Om mani padme hum,* which are rotated by hand, or even by wind or water power, to re-iterate the prayer continually; but mechanical repetition without consciousness can produce nothing. We have to learn how to sustain our prayers by our own efforts, and this is not easy. One difficulty is that we tend to make our requests too large, and ask for far more than we can be given, far more than we have any hope of paying for. Let us start with small things which are possible within the limit of our being. This is one of the things we have to observe – what is possible in our being.

So, find a practical aim and then repeat it, not mechanically, not just when we think about it, but constantly. We have to learn how to use the events of the day as opportunities for re-affirmation of the prayer and if we manage to do this there will be a complete change of quality. We shall find ourselves briefly in a new territory in which our petty worries and anxieties no longer exist, a territory scintillating with impressions of a different order from those of life.

We cannot remain in this state, nor must we expect to do so because it is the repetition of the effort which constitutes the payment. The question is whether we have anything in our being which can retain the vivid new impressions; because unless we have we shall remember nothing. So we have to organise something which can remember, something which is often likened to a cup which has to be held upright to receive the precious wine, and must be kept upright lest the contents be spilt. Again we have this important requirement of preparation. One must be ready in anticipation, must put oneself in a state where if the prayer is answered then the response may be preserved. But this receptacle which one offers up must be empty and free from the contamination of the Personality. The associations and attitudes of life must be completely set aside. One has to give up something in order to make room for something more precious and it is just the surrender of our habitual, comfortable attitudes that we find so difficult.

15

The Presence of God

The other day a thought came to me which said, 'How close are you to God?' This is not a question which we are accustomed to ask. We have an innate belief in the existence of a Supreme Deity but feel that this is something utterly remote and unattainable. Yet Christ said, 'The Kingdom of God is within you'; and we are told to try to raise our level of consciousness so that we may communicate with higher levels.

Consciousness of what? Surely what we are seeking is to be conscious in the Universe to which we belong and in which we have a purpose. Hence it will be appropriate to bring together some of our ideas about this mysterious environment. The astronomers, looking at the heavens through their telescopes, tell us that this earth is an insignificant planet in one of 10,000 million solar systems in the galaxy called the Milky Way; and that even this is only one of some 1,000 million galaxies in the vast realms of space. What on earth are we doing in this wilderness?

Esoteric cosmology takes a different view – a view from the top. It says that the Universe is brought into being by the will of a Supreme Creator, of inconceivable and ineffable intelligence, through a series of world-orders of increasingly detailed manifestation. The process is depicted in the familiar diagram called the Ray of Creation which shows how successive materialisations develop by the progressive application of the Law of Three.

We have seen that because of this sequence each world-order is directed not only by its own intelligence but is also subject to the laws of all the higher orders, so that the whole creation is a living structure continuously vivified by the influence of the Absolute which permeates all the inferior levels. It is important to realise that the successive world-orders are not separate entities but are, like the limbs of the body, parts of a coherent whole which *is* the Deity.

There is an important corollary of this idea, namely that each world-order is not only subject to the laws of its parents but is actually impregnated with the materials of the higher levels. We usually interpret materiality in physical terms; but we know that this is an illusion of the senses. The familiar substances are really loose assemblies of tiny disturbances of the void called electrons separated by relatively enormous distances. These interfere with the passage of light waves and so create the appearances of solidity and colour.

Within this virtually empty space there is clearly room for vibrations of a finer quality, which will not be detected by the ordinary senses but may have a significant influence on our behaviour. We can, moreover, envisage that the higher world-orders are similar structures involving progressively finer vibrations, so that each will possess its own materiality; and each level will be impregnated with the vibrations of all the superior orders.

This is sometimes expressed in terms of a structure of atoms, using the word in a psychological sense as the smallest particle of materiality of any given world-order. In these terms the Ray of Creation may be developed as a progressive assembly of atoms of the Absolute, as in Fig. 11. Every atom of World 3 will contain three such atoms. The atoms of the galaxy will contain six, while each atom of Solar material will contain twelve, and so on. This formulation conveys very clearly the way in which each world-order is saturated with materials of all the levels above.

Clearly these materials are not of the quality of physical

		Atome of the Absolute	
Absolute	•	1	
All worlds	⋯	3	Scale of man
Galaxy	⋮⋮	6	God
Sun	⋮⋮⋮⋮	12	Real I
Planets		24	Essence
Earth		48	Body and Personality
Moon		96	

Figure 11

substances. They can best be regarded as manifestations of the intelligence of conscious beings. Thus World 48, the level of Earth, is an intelligent being concerned with the maintenance of the physical conditions of this planet and its associated psychological activities. This we take entirely for granted. Only very occasionally do we recognise the remarkably competent directing intelligence which is operating behind the scenes.

There is a still further intelligence involved. We regard the earth as a permanent structure but actually all its constituents are coming into being at this very moment, because the (physical) atoms, having fulfilled their purpose and used their energy, die and have to be replaced. The whole of the physical earth, including the body, is a structure of continual death and replacement. Something has to organise this, has to maintain the process in operation, and this is the intelligence of World 48, responding to programmes laid down by World 24.

World 24 is an intelligence of a higher order possessing an additional degree of freedom, an extra dimension. We are familiar with the three dimensions of space, which are simply frameworks by which we can measure extensions of length, breadth and height. To the intelligence of World 24 the passing time of the senses is simply a movement along an already-existing fourth dimension, which is an integral part of the structure. It is this four-dimensional world which contains the underlying pattern of all the events and appearances of World 48. It is for us the domain of Eternity because it is not subject to the laws of passing time. Hence all the events of our world are simply manifestations in sequence of an already-existing pattern in the domain of Eternity. We have to begin to be a little aware of the existence of this level of intelligence which is called World 24, the Astral world, and which possesses its own materiality of a finer quality than that of the physical world.

It is of this material that Essence is created. This, as we know, is the spiritual part of a man which inhabits and uses the physical body. Do you feel the presence of Essence as something alive, as something of a quality utterly different from life? It is something composed of four-dimensional material, living in the realm of Eternity, so that its potentialities are vast in comparison with anything that our ordinary knowledge can contrive.

Yet this is only the lowest level of the spirit. We are told that Essence has come down – or rather, comes down, because it is happening now – comes down from the stars, from the level of World 6, the level of the Galaxy. It comes down to earth for a purpose, to utilise the energies and conditions which exist at the level of World 48 and in its descent it is partly clothed successively in materials of the worlds that it passes through. So it first acquires some of the material of World 12 and then again of World 24, at which point we call it Essence; and it is then provided with a physical body through which it can explore the conditions of World 48, the phenomenal world.

Evidently a man (or a woman) is a creation of much larger stature than the physical body, much greater than the Personality with all its cleverness, all its intellect. It is something which contains as part of its very structure all these higher intelligences. This is sometimes put up in the following form :

WORLD 6   GOD
WORLD 12   REAL I
WORLD 24   ESSENCE
WORLD 48   PERSONALITY (Body)

God for us is not the Absolute, because this intelligence, and that of World 3, are utterly beyond our comprehension. For us, God is the intelligence of World 6. The important thing is that all these intelligences, all these materials, actually exist in the structure called man. In his state of sleep he is just not aware of this. He lives entirely in the basement, is not even aware of the magnificence and delicacy of Essence which he dimly perceives, or conceives to exist within him, without any real understanding of the enormous difference of quality and potentiality of this spiritual element.

However, as said, this is only the lowest level of the spirit. There is in us material of an even finer nature, of the quality of World 12. This is called Real I, an entity possessing objective consciousness which can communicate with the Solar level of intelligence. This we know little about, but usually associate it with what we imagine to be our real self. We tend to think of it, perhaps, as some extra-intelligent I of Personality. We are told to observe the cage of I's, rather like a cage of monkeys, containing the thousands of automata which conduct our affairs for us; and because some of these can respond to conscious influences we have the illusion that out of them may one day develop Real I.

Real I is of an utterly different quality, incommensurable with the I's of Personality, which are created by life. Real I is a spiritual creation which is 'within hail' of God. But we are told that it is not permanent in us. It may briefly exercise control of our behaviour, but can only do so for any length of time as a result of hard and persistent work on oneself.

Yet the material is there, together with the even finer substances of World 6. The whole of the structure, indeed, is permeated by this exquisite material, so that the divine spirit exists and is present in man at all his levels.

So if we ask how close we are to God the answer is in our own hands. The material is there to be acknowledged, not as a starry-eyed vision but as a practical exercise.

I was reminded recently of the prayer, 'God be in my head', so beautifully set to music by Sir Walford Davies, which seems to summarise exactly what we are talking about. It originates from the Sarum Primer of 1558, a collection of ideas by the early monks of the period and runs, you will remember :

> God be in my head
> And in my understanding.
> God be in mine eyes
> And in my looking.
> God be in my mouth
> And in my speaking.
> God be in my heart
> And in my thinking.
> God be at mine end
> And at my departing.

We usually hear this inspiring prayer only at funerals but it is a prayer for living. It is a prayer of self-remembering, a prayer that God, this ineffable intelligence of World 6 which is in me, may actually be present in all the activities of my daily life. The whole of our being is impregnated with all the levels of consciousness available to us, from World 6 downwards, but in an undeveloped state.

Once we understand the potentialities of this idea we know why we have to make effort – not because we are told to, but because we want to inhabit the whole of this magnificent structure. How can we speak of this in words? Only the emotional mind can perceive the truth; but if this is acknowledged, we may perhaps find the secret which was discovered by the mediaeval monk Brother Lawrence – a very humble member of his order, who nevertheless did everything that was required of him 'in the presence of God'.

APPENDIX

The Fourth Way

The fulfilment of the life can be attempted in various ways. Some seek it through physical mastery, others by religious observance, while yet others submit to the disciplines of yoga. Each of these ways is concerned with the development of a particular Centre, involving persistent effort, usually to the exclusion of life interests. There is, however, a Fourth Way, as taught by Gurdjieff, which is designed to stimulate a balanced use of all the Centres. This requires a conscious participation in the events of the day rather than an attempt to escape from them, and it can lead to an entirely new understanding of life.

The ideas of the Fourth Way are clear and precise; to practise them is a different matter. It is a task for which one needs help because the customary associations of habit are quite inadequate. One is, in fact, venturing into unknown territory beyond the confines of ordinary experience. So one has to rely on notes left by people who have made this journey before, which fortunately are available for those who choose to use them.

The important requirement, however, is to set sail. One can spend one's time in an avid pursuit of fresh knowledge instead of trying to use what one already has, which is like buying innumerable tickets to China without ever leaving the comfort of one's fireside. We must not wait until we feel ready because we do not know what we really need. We shall make many abortive excursions, but from each something can be learned. Gradually a new understanding will begin to crystallise within oneself and when this happens one may find, apparently by accident, a teacher from whom individual assistance can be obtained.

There are, in fact, many schools throughout the world concerned with the practical application of the Fourth Way. They do not advertise, for they are open only to those who have developed more than a casual interest in the ideas and have made some effort to discover a suitable teacher.

In such a school one can be shown, and made to work on, aspects of one's being to which the customary self-esteem is totally blind, and can develop new relationships to other people, and to the Universe. But this does not absolve one from the need to make individual effort. There is indeed an increased obligation and many fall by the wayside because they are unwilling to sacrifice their complacency.

For those who contemplate embarking on this journey reference may be made to the following works which embrace the basic tenets of the system.

In Search of the Miraculous by P. D. Ouspensky (Routledge) An account of his eight years with Gurdjieff, including a detailed synthesis of the cosmology.

Psychological Commentaries on the teaching of Gurdjieff and Ouspensky by Maurice Nicoll (Watkins) A series of papers written for his groups during the years from 1941 to his death in 1953.

The Fourth Way by P. D. Ouspensky (Routledge) A symposium of questions and answers in his groups between 1921 and 1946.

All & Everything by G. I. Gurdjieff (Routledge) An allegorical presentation of secret knowledge of the Universe and man's situation therein, written as a series of tales told by Beelzebub to his grandson about his several visits to the planet Earth.

The New Man by Maurice Nicoll (Watkins) An interpretation of some of the parables and miracles of Christ as clues to the development of the inner man.

There is much additional literature but any extensive biblio-
graphy is irrelevant until one has assimilated the basic ideas and
begun to apply them to oneself. For the same reason it would be
inappropriate to supply a detailed list of available schools. The
principal centres of the teaching are

The Gurdjieff Centre 11 Addison Crescent London W 14.

The Gurdjieff Foundation 123 East 63rd Street New York 10021
NY.

Societe d'etudes pour la connaissance de l'homme 5 Rue du Col
Marchand Paris 16e.

The Church of the Earth (Dr Robert S. Ropp) Sonoma County,
California.

Index

Absolute 3, 15, 29, 89, 97, 106
Active force 15, 62, 83
Ascending octaves 66, 79
Associations 3, 7, 21, 37, 50, 96
Astral body 34, 53
Astral world 17, 24, 36, 44, 83, 92, 108
Atoms 18, 48, 106
Attention 10, 47, 51, 80
Attitudes 61, 85, 98, 103
Aura 53
Automaton 21, 50

Behaviour unit 21
Being 22, 39, 47, 96, 103
Body, physical 10, 23, 93, 108
Brain 7, 10, 27
Breath, time of 90
Breathing, function of 80

Cancelling 60
Carbon 71
Cellular world 79, 91
Centres 30, 73, 80
Centres, speeds of 75
Changing the past 46, 85
Characteristic times 90
Chief Feature 59
Conscious circle of humanity 14
Conscious influences 4, 20, 35, 83, 96
Conscious shock 83
Conscious use of events 11, 24, 38
Consciousness, illusion of 11, 20
Considering 58
Cosmic dance 72
Cosmoses 79, 88
Creative octaves 66

Daily bread 99
Day and night 14, 90
Death 107
Debts 60, 99
Deity 105

Descending octaves 67
Difficulties, use of 63, 100
Digestion 64, 78
Digestion of impressions 83
Dimensions 91, 97, 107
Discontinuity 71, 80, 88, 97

Effort 4, 10, 25, 52, 63, 87, 96, 101
Emotional Centre 32, 53
Emotional mind 12, 24, 76, 94
Enabling force 62
Esoteric influences 11, 14, 25
Essence 8, 23, 29, 36, 100, 108
Eternity 8, 26, 44, 92, 108
Evolution 5, 18, 91
Expanded awareness 52, 86, 93
Expectation 11, 17, 24, 43
External considering 60

Fabric of eternity 39, 44
False Personality 11, 43, 57, 87
Fear 23
Feeling of I 21, 57, 101
First conscious shock 83
Forces 15, 62
Formatory mind 34, 45
Fourth body 54
Freedom 25, 43, 97
Fruit 86

Galaxy 13, 49, 108
Gratitude 14, 60
Greater Mind 29
Group minds 2
Guilt, feeling of 23, 38, 59

Harmony 9, 32, 64
Heaven 11, 24, 93
Higher bodies 48, 87
Higher Centres 33, 74
Hydrogens, concept of 71
Hydrogens, function of 74
Hypnotism of life 1, 20

115

Index

Side octave 67
Sin 22
Sleep 10, 23, 50, 109
Solar level 17, 49, 54, 66
Songs, habitual 58
Soul 39, 49
Stillness 26
Sun intelligence 17

Temptation 100
Third body 54
Third force 15, 62, 101
Three, law of 15, 62
Thought 25, 51, 75
Time 15, 41, 70
Time body 44, 85
Time scales 35, 44, 88
Tonic Sol-fa 64

Transformation 38, 52, 64, 78
Translation 23, 53
Triads 63

Uses, doctrine of 23, 71
Understanding 12, 24, 35, 46, 52, 60, 83, 98
Unmanifest world 3, 8, 28, 45

Value, scale of 70
Vibrations 3, 64, 71, 106
Vital energy 53, 73, 80

Wedding garment 101
Waking and sleeping 90
Wonder, sense of 1, 12
World orders 3, 16, 49, 88, 97, 105